THE ARABS
A SHORT HISTORY

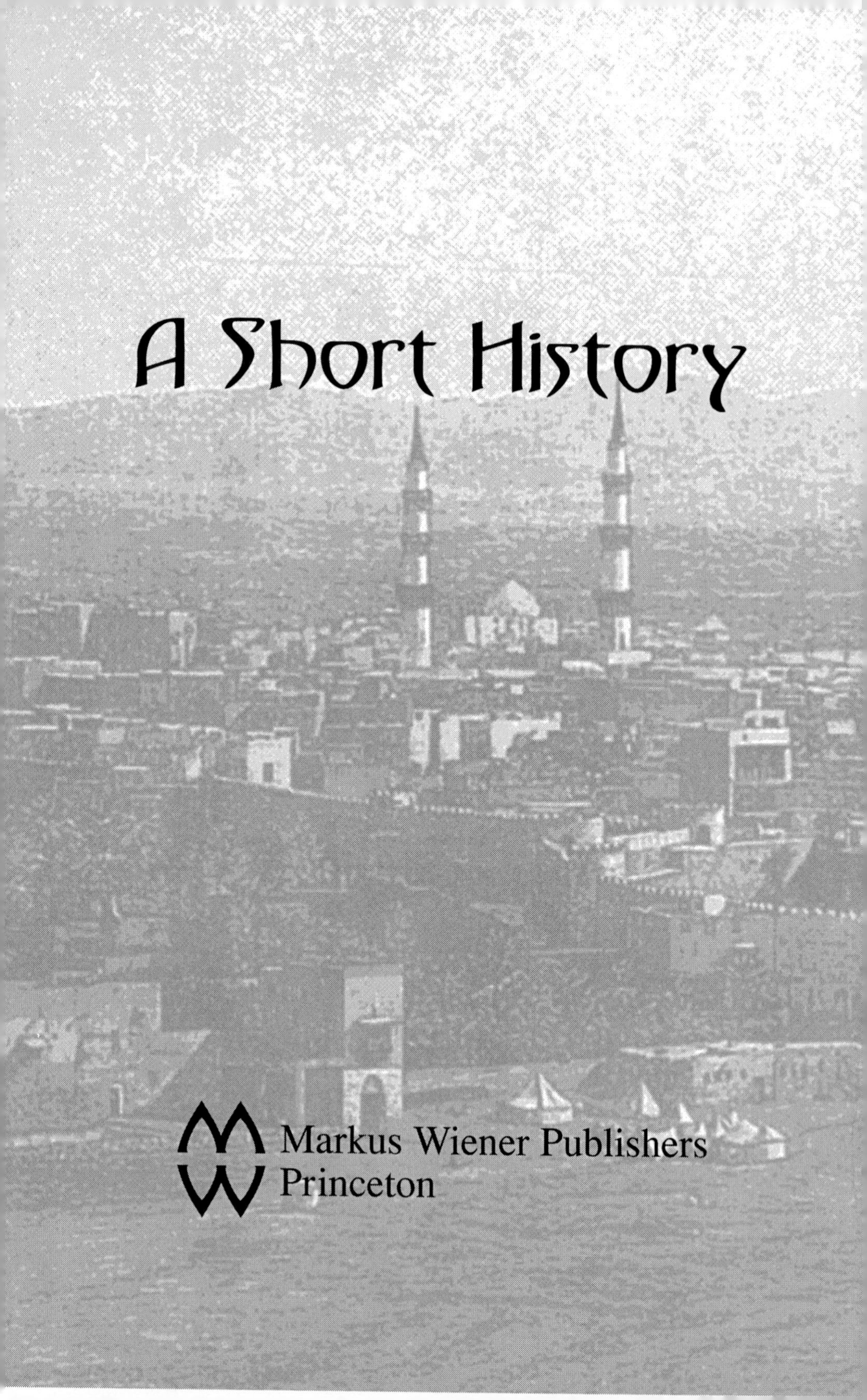

A Short History

Markus Wiener Publishers
Princeton

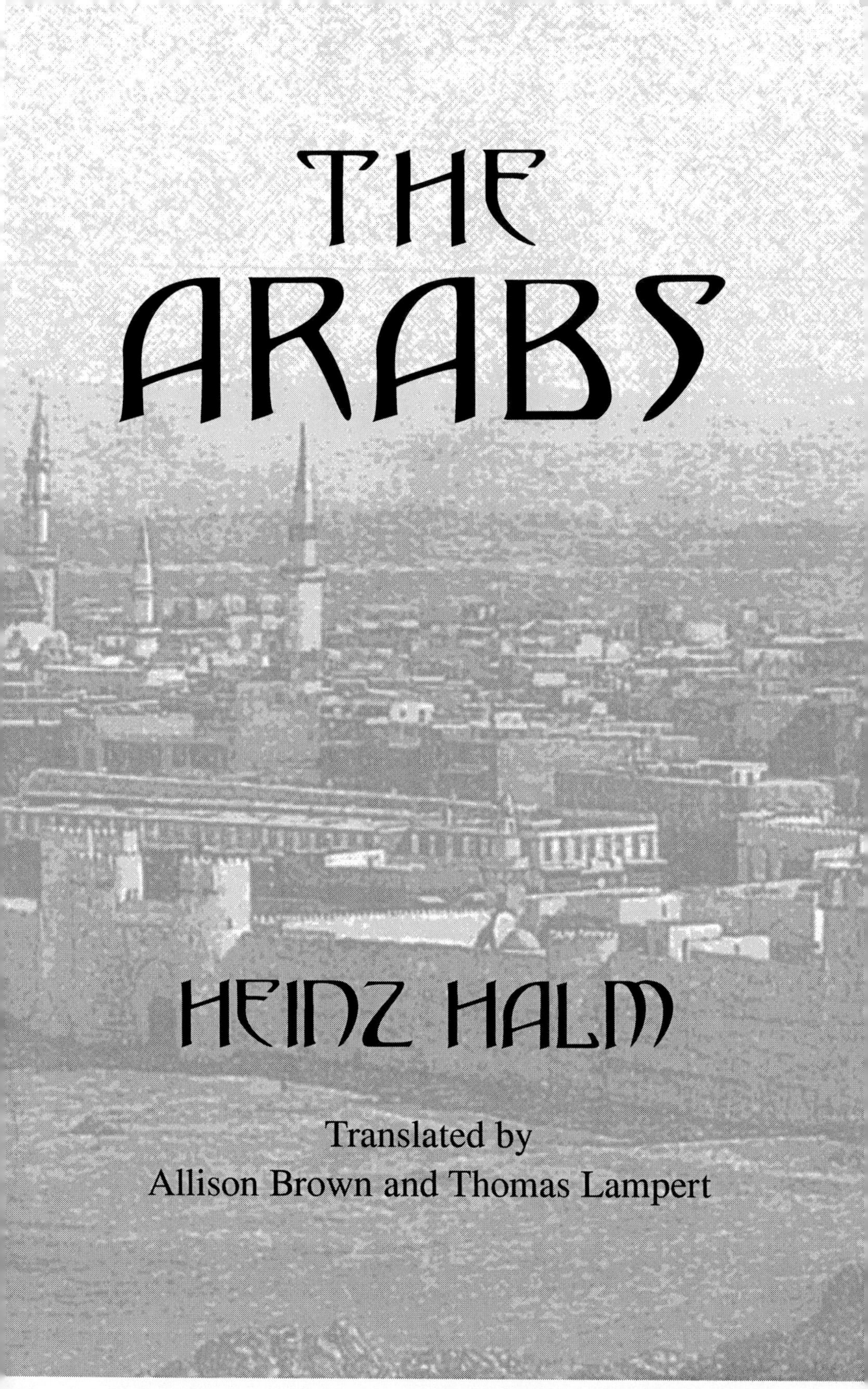

THE ARABS

HEINZ HALM

Translated by
Allison Brown and Thomas Lampert

Translated from German by Allison Brown and Thomas Lampert.
The translation of this work was supported by the Goethe-Institut.

For information write to:
Markus Wiener Publishers
231 Nassau Street, Princeton, NJ 08542
www.markuswiener.com

Library of Congress Cataloging-in-Publication Data

Halm, Heinz, 1942-
[Araber. English]
The Arabs : a short history / Heinz Halm.
p. cm.
Includes bibliographical references and index.
ISBN-13: 978-1-55876-416-3 (hardcover : alk. paper)
ISBN-10: 1-55876-416-X (hardcover : alk. paper)
1. Arabs—History. 2. Arab countries—History. I. Title.
DS37.7.H3513 2007
909'.04927—dc22

2006029943

Printed in the United States of America on acid-free paper

Table of Contents

1

Pre-Islamic Arabia

Ruins of the Mārib dam

From Klaus Shippman, *Ancient South Arabia* (Princeton: Markus Wiener, 2001)

Name and Origin

Arabs call themselves *al-'Arab*, a collective term used to designate the Arab people as a whole. *Al-'Arabī* is the term for an individual member of that people. This affiliation is based first of all on the use of the Arabic language: An Arab is someone who speaks Arabic. There are approximately 280 million Arabic-speaking people in North Africa and the Middle East today, from the Atlantic Ocean to the western edge of the Iranian plateau, that is, from Morocco and Mauritania in the west to Iraq in the east, and from Syria in the north to Oman, Yemen, and Sudan in the south. This expansion of the Arab people and the Arabic language is a relatively recent historical phenomenon related to the spread of Islam beginning in the seventh century CE.

The first known use of the term Arab is found in an inscription of the Assyrian king Shalmaneser III from 853 BCE celebrating a victory of the Assyrians over the coalition of Syrian kings (including the King of Israel) at the Battle of Qarqar in Syria. According to the inscription, the Syrian coalition was supported by a contingent of a thousand camel riders of Gindibu, King of the Arabs (*Aribi*). Inscriptions of Assyrian kings from the eighth and seventh centuries BCE repeatedly mention kings and queens of the Arabs, for the most part as tributaries and auxiliary forces of the Assyrians.

The *Aribi* mentioned in Assyrian inscriptions appear to

have been nomadic groups living in the Syrian Desert, in other words, on the inner margins of the Fertile Crescent (Palestine/Jordan, Syria, and Iraq). As Shalmaneser III's inscription indicates, the name *Aribi* was from the beginning tied to the use of dromedaries. As pack and riding animals but also as sources of meat and wool, these animals enabled human life in the desert steppe (*bādiya*). It is from the latter term that Arab nomads or Bedouins derive their name (*al-badawī*). Numerous Assyrian reliefs from the era of King Sennacherib (705–681 BCE) depict Arabic camel riders in battle. For the Assyrians, whose imperial claims included all of Syria, controlling the Arabs of the Syrian Desert was of great strategic importance.

There were no significant changes in the Neo-Babylonian Empire after the fall of Nineveh in 612 BCE. Nabonidus, the final king of Babylon (556–539 BCE), even continued to live for ten years in the palace he had built in the northwestern Arabian oasis of Taimā, leaving Babylon to his son Belshazzar, the crown prince. His sphere of control extended to Yathrib, which later became known as Medina. After 549 BCE, Persian kings do not appear to have ruled the Arabs directly, but rather to have sought them as allies. Herodotus reported (III, 88) that before the Persian king Cambyses conquered Egypt in 525 BCE, he obtained consent from the Arabs. Xerxes also used Arabs as archers on camelback during his campaign against Greece (480 BCE) (VII, 69; 86).

Almost all of these reports portray the *Aribi* as inhabitants of the inner periphery of the Fertile Crescent in the Syrian-Mesopotamian desert and in northern Arabia, where they initially appeared as nomadic camel herders, but also as farmers in the oases of northwestern Arabia. It is here that the name "Arab" appears for the first time (we do not know the origin of the term), and it is here as well that the (North) Arabic language – the bond that continues to unite the Arab people – has its roots.

Arabic is one of the Semitic languages, a language family named after Shem, the son of Noah, according to the Table of Nations in the Old Testament (Genesis 10) the progenitor of both the people of Israel and the Arabs. Arabic is thus closely related to the languages spoken in the Fertile Crescent during antiquity (Akkadian = Babylonian/Assyrian, Phoenician, Canaanite, Hebrew, and Aramaic), as well as to Old South Arabic and the languages of Abyssinia (Ethiopian, Tigre, Tigrinya, and Amharic). The oldest evidence of the (North) Arabic language are brief inscriptions found at the oases extending like a chain of pearls from the south of present-day Jordan through the Ḥijāz and down to ʻAsīr. Such graffiti has been documented since the era of Assyrian rule. It was initially written in alphabets that were closely related to Old South Arabic and that developed – like Greek and Latin – from a Phoenician prototype. The Arabic alphabet used today thus has the same roots as our Latin alphabet, even if its appearance would hardly suggest it. As this alphabet had less than thirty letters to denote spoken phonemes, it spread across the entire Middle East, replacing the much more complicated writing forms of the ancient Orient, cuneiform scripts and hieroglyphics.

Ancient South Arabia

The territory that constitutes present-day Yemen lay outside the Assyrian Empire's sphere of influence, although the kings of Sheba are occasionally mentioned in Assyrian inscriptions. With 10,000-foot mountain peaks and heavy monsoon rains, the southwest of the Arabian Peninsula is a world onto itself. The ancient landscapes here of terraced fields and stonewalled cities present a marked contrast to the rest of the peninsula. Since time immemorial, people in this area had mediated trade between the Indian Ocean and the Mediterranean. In particular, frankincense (a tree resin) extracted around Dhofār in present-day Oman was traded through the kingdoms of South Arabia to the north, where large amounts were used in temples and later in churches of the Middle East and Greece. The Incense Road led from Dhofār through several dominions that, while not producing any incense themselves, controlled and thereby profited from the trade in it: Ḥaḍramawt, and west of this Qatabān with its capital of Timna'; Sheba with its capital Mārib; and Ma'īn with its cities in al-Jawf (northeast of San'ā'). The Old Testament tells of the Queen of Sheba (almost certainly a legendary figure) who is said to have visited King Solomon in Jerusalem. Sheba and Ḥaḍramawt (*Hasarmaweth*) also appear in the Table of Nations in the Old Testament (Genesis 10).

The Kingdom of Ma'īn, which can be documented from approximately 550 to 125 BCE, extended at times into northwestern Arabia. It established a trade colony in Dedan (present-day al-'Ulā) in the fourth century BCE, and its merchants reached Egypt and Syria. At times Ma'īn fell under the rule of neighboring Sheba. Karib'il Watar, the king of Sheba from approximately 510 to 490 BCE, had his conquests immortalized in victory inscriptions. The Old South Arabic language, like modern Arabic a Semitic language, had its own written alphabet. Several thousand inscriptions provide us with insight into the culture of Sheba. Numerous large buildings such as temples have survived in the capital Mārib. However, the most important construction here was the Great Dam of Mārib, approximately 2000 feet long, which was used to dam the waters of the Wādī Adhana between two mountain ridges. A complicated system of locks and canals was used to irrigate the entire region around the capital city.

Arabia in the Hellenistic Period

Alexander the Great did not touch Arabia during his military campaign. However, Alexander's admiral Nearchus, on his return from India through Cape Musandam, did reach the northern point of what is today Oman, before leading his fleet back to Mesopotamia through the gulf. Alexander's own plans for oceanic exploration were interrupted by his early death in 323 BCE. Of Alexander's wealthy successors or Diadochi – the Seleucids in Syria/Mesopotamia and the Ptolemaeans in Egypt – especially the latter had close ties to Arabia, as they exercised maritime control over the Red Sea. The Greeks were familiar with the southern Arabian kingdoms of Ḥaḍramawt, Qatabān, Sheba, and Maʿīn. Greek geographers mentioned their capital cities and the Chatramotitai, Kattabaneis, Sabaioi, and Minaioi peoples – the last named were the Minaeans from Maʿīn.

Most of the surviving inscriptions written in the precursors of present-day (North) Arabic were created during the Hellenistic period. This includes several thousand inscriptions, most of which are brief graffiti etched in rocks, in which travelers immortalized their presence or called for assistance from certain gods. While these inscriptions are written in alphabets derived from Old South Arabic (Sabaean), the language is clearly North Arabic and thus has been designated as proto-Arabic. The two most significant of these written forms are Lihyanic and Thamudic. Both written forms have been dated from at least the fifth century BCE up into the Common Era. Thamudic graffiti has been found throughout the entire Ḥijāz and 'Asīr, the Sinai, southern Palestine, and Transjordan.

The Nabataeans were also Arabs. Their capital city Petra was located in a rocky basin east of the Dead Sea. The first historical reports of the Nabataeans appear directly after the death of Alexander the Great. In 312 BCE, Antigonus, one of Alexander's generals, attempted to take Petra. The Nabataeans controlled the Incense Road to the east of their city. Antigonus had taken spoils of frankincense and spices in Petra, and the Roman historian Diodorus expressly noted that the Nabataeans transported frankincense and myrrh to the Mediterranean Sea. However, they also engaged in piracy on the Red Sea, which led to conflicts with the Ptolemaeans in Egypt. The Nabataeans gradually brought the entire Transjordan and southern Palestine including Gaza under their control. The Nabataean King Aretas III (in Arabic *al-Ḥāritha*, 87–62 BCE) was even able to take control of Damascus in 85 BCE. Although the Nabataeans spoke Arabic, as indicated by the names of their kings, they employed a script developed from the Aramaic alphabet for their correspondence and inscriptions. The Nabataeans' material culture was also influenced by the north, as is evident even today in the impressive Hellenistic fak̲ades of the rock tombs of Petra. The epithet of Aretas III was *Philhellenos*, or friend of Greece.

The Greeks' familiarity with Arabia during the Hellenistic period is also evident in the work of the geographer Ptolemy of Alexandria (second century BCE), which maps the entire Arabian Peninsula including the interior.

Arabs and Romans

The Roman proconsul Pompey traveled to Syria in 64 BCE in order to reorganize political relations in the Levant along Roman lines. In the preceding year, Roman troops had driven the Nabataean king Aretas III out of Damascus and occupied the city. Pompey now transformed Syria into a Roman province. In 63 BCE, Pompey himself advanced from Antioch through Damascus to Jericho and Jerusalem. He permitted the small Jewish kingdom of the Hasmoneans and the Nabataean kingdom to exist as Roman client states, content to have subjugated the Middle East to the *Pax Romana*. The subsequent Roman civil wars were often fought in Asia Minor. After Octavian (Augustus) annexed Ptolemaic Egypt in 30 BCE, Roman influence extended also to the Red Sea.

Like the Greeks before them, the Romans distinguished between *Arabia Deserta* or "Desert Arabia" and the "happy" *Arabia Felix*, Yemen. This epithet is the result of a misunderstanding of an Arabic term. For Arabs, who were "oriented" to the east, the south lay to the "right" (*al-Yaman*) and the north lay to the "left" (*al-Shām*). In contemporary Arabic these two words are still used to designate Yemen and Syria. Yemen, in other words, is actually the land "on the right side." However, "right" also means "propitious," and in this way the "land to the right" became "happy Arabia" (*Arabia eudaimon* in Greek). The name, however, could also be understood in a different sense: The luxury goods that Romans so desired came from here. According to the geographers Strabo and Pliny the Elder, *Arabia Felix* or Yemen was the Roman source for incense and myrrh, cassia and nard, silk, jewels, and pearls – that is, products not produced in Yemen itself but in southeastern Arabia or beyond the Indian Ocean and the Persian Gulf in India and China. Augustus' decision to send a military expedition into "happy Arabia" in 24–25 BCE was probably motivated above all by his desire to control trade in these goods. A Roman official, Aelius Gallus, commanded the Roman troops, ostensibly ten thousand in number. Syllaios, the minister of the Nabataean king, assumed leadership of the expedition, and the Nabataean king and the Jewish king Herod provided auxiliary forces. The troops were transported on 130 cargo ships from the Gulf of Suez to Leuke Kome (Yanbu'), and from there they made the grueling march through 'Asīr. They conquered Najrān and the cities of Ma'īn, but had to abandon the siege of Mārib after six days due to lack of water. The Roman army was forced to withdrawal with significant losses. The geographer Strabo, who was acquainted with Aelius Gallus, recorded the various stages of the march.

The enterprise was a complete disaster both militarily and politically, although there was no significant political force in Yemen at the time and city princes ruled the country. However, a new force was rising in the south of Yemen: the tribe of the Himyarites, whose capital city Ẓafār with the citadel Dhū Raydān (75 miles south of San'ā) now became the main city of *Arabia Felix*. Immediately after Aelius Gallus' failed campaign, old Sheba and the new Himyarites joined to form the "Kingdom of Sheba and Dhū

Raydān." This new kingdom successively subsumed the smaller kingdoms of Ma'īn, Qatabān, and Ḥaḍramawt. The *Homeritae*, as the Romans called the Himyarites, ruled southern Arabia during the entire Roman imperial era. Trade relations between the two empires seem to have remained close, and the Romans never again attempted to take direct control of *Arabia Felix*.

The situation was different in northern Arabia. Here Arabs were not only the immediate neighbors of the Roman province of Syria, but they also lived in increasing numbers within the Roman Empire itself. Nomads moved between the villages on the edge of the Syrian Desert, occasionally settling permanently there or in one of the cities. Arabs trickled into the settled areas of the Fertile Crescent in the same way that Semitic-speaking peoples – the Akkadians, Aramaeans, Canaanites, and the Israelites – had done for thousands of years. Under the Seleucids, the Itureans (*Itouraioi*), who were almost certainly South Arabian, had pushed into Galilee in the second century BCE and taken control of the Beqā' plain between Lebanon and Antilebanon. Safā inscriptions, Arabic graffiti in the Safā Hills southeast of Damascus, from the first century BCE to the fourth century CE testify to the presence of Arabs there. In 70 CE, after the destruction of Jerusalem by Titus, Judea became a Roman province, and in 106 CE, Emperor Trajan also annexed the Nabataean kingdom, turning it into the Roman province Arabia. In this way, the entire western horn of the Fertile Crescent was incorporated into the Roman Empire. In the autumn of 129 CE, Emperor Hadrian visited Palmyra, Damascus, Beirut, and Petra, before spending the winter in Gerasa (Jerash in northern Jordan).

Emperor Philip the Arab (244–249) was born in the Jabal el Druze in a hamlet that he renamed Philippopolis (present-day Shahba, fifty miles southeast of Damascus), in which he built a theater and other magnificent structures.

Further northeast, the oasis city of Palmyra (*Tadmur* in Arabic), which owed its ascent as a trade city to the decline of Petra, gradually became Arabized. The rulers, who attempted to establish a vast Middle-Eastern empire between the Roman and the Parthian empires in the third century, had Arabic names: Odaenathus (*'Udhayna*), his bride Zenobia (*Zaynab*), and their son "Augustus" Vaballathus (*Wahb Allāt* = "Gift of the Goddess Allāt"). Emperor Aurelius ended the Palmyrians' imperial dreams in 272, bringing Zenobia and her son to Rome as captives.

Like Palmyra, Hatra in northern Mesopotamia also flourished in the second and third centuries as a result of its location at the border between the Roman and the Parthian empires and its function as a trade emporium. The city had a predominantly Arab population. It was not far from the Tigris (60 miles southwest of Mosul) but had never belonged to the Parthian Empire and had successfully resisted Roman legions, both those of Emperor Trajan (117 CE) and those of Septimius Severus (197 CE). Not until 240 CE were the Persians able to take the city.

Arabia between Byzantines and Persians

Two events outside of Arabia marked epochal changes for Arabs as well. In 226 CE, the Persian king Ardashir ended Parthian rule of Iran and Mesopotamia. The new ruler assumed the old title of *King of Kings*, establishing a Sassanid Neo-Persian Empire. The Parthian royal city of Ctesiphon on the Tigris (25 miles southeast of present-day Baghdad) became the residence of the new great kings. In 330 CE, the Roman Emperor Constantine established his capital city of Constantinople on the site of the old Greek city Byzantium, which became the new metropolis of the Eastern Roman Empire. As a result, the Syrian Desert and the Arabian Peninsula became an area of conflict for these two neighboring major powers of late antiquity, which clashed here in the north as well as in the south.

The Arabic Lakhmid tribe established their rule west of the lower Euphrates around 300 CE. The Lakhmid kingdom served the Persian Empire as a buffer state against the Eastern Roman Empire. The royal residence of the Lakhmids was al-Ḥīra (from the Aramaic *Herta* or "camp"; cf. Hatra), which was located south of what later became Kūfa (present-day Najaf). We know of more than twenty Lakhmid kings up to the beginning of the seventh century. The grave stelae for Imru al-Qays (died in 328), designating him as the "King of all Arabs," have been uncovered in Ḥawrān in Syria. Al-Nu'mān I (ca. 400–418) built magnificent castles, including the fabulous al-Khawarnaq Palace near al-Ḥīra, which has survived in the legends and poems of later eras. As a vassal of the Sassanids, al-Mundhir III (ca. 505–554), a contemporary of Justinian, engaged in raids against Byzantine Syria, which brought him into the vicinity of Antioch. His son ʻAmr (554–569) is renowned as the patron of poets. At least three of the seven most important pre-Islamic Arab poets are reputed to have lived at his court. His mother was Christian and founded a monastery in al-Ḥīra. Starting in the early fifth century, there was a bishop in the city, although in all probability only the final Lakhmid king, al-Nuʻmān III (ca. 580–602), was himself a Nestorian Christian.

The Arab buffer state on the Byzantine side, in which the Banū Gassān clan shielded the Syrian provinces from the desert, is much younger. The center of the Ghassānid kingdom was Jābiya in Jawlān (Golan), a cross between a nomadic camp and a settled city. There were also palatial buildings along the edge of the desert steppe, where the Ghassānids could receive the leaders of allied tribes. As vassals of Byzantium, they were Christians, although they belonged to the Monophysite (Jacobite) Church predominant in Syria. The Ghassānids reached the apex of their power in the sixth century. In 529, Emperor Justinian named al-Ḥārith II (ca. 529–569) *phylarchos* and gave him the title *patricius*, making him one of the highest dignitaries in the Roman Empire. Justinian prepared a magnificent reception for him in Constantinople in 563. His son al-Mundhir (*Alamundaros*) was also received at the court in 580, but the relationship subsequently deteriorated, not least because the Ghassānids refused to abandon their "heretical" Monophysite beliefs. Al-Mundhir was finally deported to Sicily and his son al-Nu'mān was imprisoned in Constantinople. Ghassānid rule was brought to an end in 613–614, after the Sassanid king Khosrow II Parvez captured Damascus and Jerusalem. The last Ghassānid Jabala VI fought on the side of the Byzantines against the Arab Muslims in 636, but later converted to Islam.

Another battleground for the rivalry between the Byzantine and Persian Empires was Yemen. The Himyarites (*Homeritae*) had ruled over the former empire of Sheba since the third century. There was a coup around 500 CE, in which the ruling dynasty was deposed and a usurper with the epithet *Dhū Nuwās* ("he with the curl") assumed power. *Dhū Nuwās* was Jewish and called himself Yūsuf after the Biblical Joseph. Following the Roman destruction of Jerusalem in 70 CE, Judaism appears to have been spread by refugees and exiles along the Incense Road to the south and there also seems to have been some conversions among Arab tribes and clans. At the time of Muḥammad, three of the five Arabic tribes living in Yathrib (Medina) were Jewish. The Yemenite king Yūsuf /Dhū Nuwās is said to have to have persecuted the apparently large Christian population in his empire as retribution for Roman-Byzantine oppression of the Jews. In response, Christian Ethiopians, backed by Christian Byzantium, intervened. The negus or sovereign of Ethiopia conquered Yemen between 523 and 525, dethroned the persecutor of Christians, and established Christian Ethiopian viceroys as rulers, thus bringing an end to the Kingdom of Sheba and Himyar.

Abraha, one of these Ethiopian viceroys, is said to have built a magnificent church in San'ā', almost certainly on the site of today's great mosque, the famous al-Qalīs (*ekklesia* in Greek). Another epochal date in South Arabian history occurred during his reign: the final destruction of the Great Dam of Mārib. Several dam catastrophes were reported in the fifth and sixth centuries. According to one inscription, Abraha was still able to make repairs in 542. A short time later, however, the dam appears to have burst a final time, turning the lowlands of Mārib, the heartland of Sheba, into desert. The memory of this has been preserved in sura 34 of the Qur'ān, "The Sabaean" (verses 15–17). Abraha is also mentioned in sura 105, "The Elephant": He is said to have taken part in a military campaign against Mecca, in which he served as an elephant leader. According to several accounts, the "Year of the Elephant," in which God miraculously allowed the Christian assault to fail, is also the year in which the Prophet Muḥammad was born (ca. 570).

Soon after this – the entire chronology of ancient South Arabia remains sketchy – the Yemenites rose up against Ethiopian foreign rule, calling for assistance from the Persian king. The Sassanids had already established themselves on the western side of the Persian-Arabian Gulf – numerous castles in Oman can be traced back to this time – and they did not hesitate to intervene in South Arabia, thereby bringing the entire trade along the Incense Road under their control as well. King Khosrow I Anushirvan sent an army, which drove the Ethiopians out of Yemen. The Persians installed local viceroys, who administered the southern Arabian satrapy for them. Yemen remained a Persian province for almost sixty years until the Islamic conquest.

Ancient Old Arabic Language, Poetry, and Script

Three developments in the north of the Arabian Peninsula on the inner perimeter of the Fertile Crescent during the sixth century proved constitutive for the development of the Arab world: the (North) Arabic language, the Arabic script (which emerged as part of a continuing development of the Nabataean alphabet and which appears to have been used throughout northern Arabia on the eve of Islam), and ancient Arabic poetry.

The Arabic language (*al-'Arabiyya*) appears to have emerged quite suddenly in the sixth century with an already highly developed form of poetry. We have no record of the formative phases that must have preceded this. Its central form was the *qaṣīda* (a longer ode) and it possessed over a dozen complicated quantitative meters. This rich prosody was without parallel or precursor among the Semitic languages of the Fertile Crescent. The poetry had its origins in the tribal milieu. The poet (*shā'ir*), who was believed to be inspired by spirits (*jinn*), initially functioned as a representative of his tribe and his clan, celebrating his own tribe and reviling others. Praise and censure, panegyric and satire were often the subject of the qaṣīda as well, even after its content had become more diverse. In the sixth century, the poets already appeared as self-assured individuals leading an autonomous poetic existence. The influence of poets was evident not only at the great annual markets on the Arabian

Peninsula (such as in ‘Ukāẓ near Mecca), where poets competed with their rivals, but also at the Lakhmid court in al-Ḥīra and the Ghassānid court in Transjordan, where the figure of the court poet and the panegyrist appeared. The poet Nābigha, for example, can be regarded as a court poet of the king of al-Ḥīra.

Poems were presented orally. The great poets of the sixth century were often surrounded by a group of reciters or *rāwi*, who ensured the dissemination of their qaṣīdas and thus of the authors’ fame. Many poems of the pre-Islamic era were collected in the eighth century – several hundred complete qaṣīdas and countless fragments are extant – and were recorded in *dīwāns* (the word, taken from Persian, means “index” or “list”). Two of these collections are particularly noteworthy: the *Mu‘allaqāt* (literally, “the suspended or hanged,” although the precise meaning of the title has never been clarified); and the *Ḥamāsa* (“zeal,” “enthusiasm,” or “courage”) by Abū Tammām. The *Mu‘allaqāt* is comprised of ten qaṣīdas (originally seven with three added), each from a different poet. Even today, this collection is regarded as the classic model of Arabic poetry. A rāwi from the eighth century compiled the initial seven poems that constitute the basis of the collection. Three of the odes are directed at a Lakhmid king from al-Ḥīra. The *Ḥamāsa* is an anthology of pre-Islamic poetry compiled by poet Abū Tammām in the ninth century.

Arabic is an enormously rich language. With its guttural (velar) and emphatic sounds, it possesses greater phonetic diversity than English. It also has a highly differentiated system of verb forms and an enormous vocabulary with numerous synonyms and a variety of nuanced expressions,

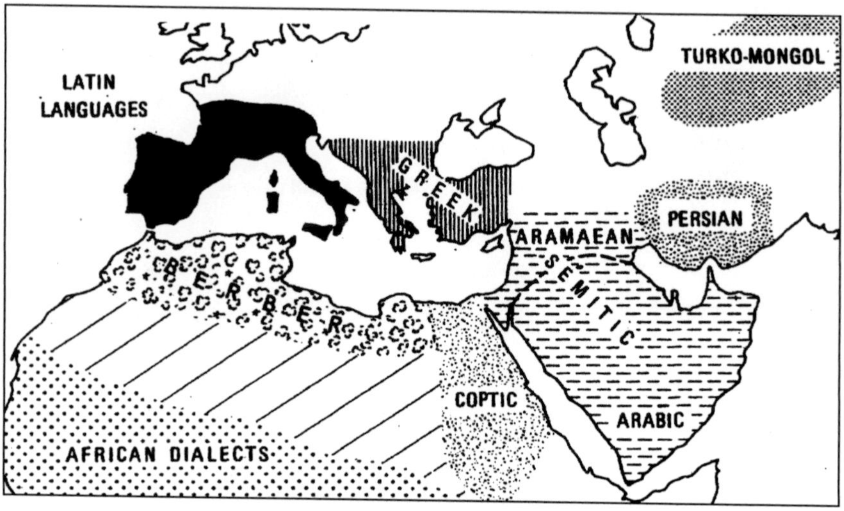

Distribution of languages before the Muslim conquests.
From Maurice Lombard, *The Golden Age of Islam* (Princeton: Markus Wiener, 2003)

such as for different types of deserts, physical peculiarities, age levels, and characteristics of cattle. One reason for this enormous variety might be the tendency and ability often attributed to Arabs (not without some justification) of becoming intoxicated with the melodiousness of their own language.

The Arabic script consists of twenty-eight letters, all of which are consonants. (Short vowels are not written, and long ones are only implied.) Most of these letters, however, have a different form depending on whether they appear at the beginning, middle, or end of a word, or whether they appear alone. This rich variety of letters also lends itself to ornamental decoration, which has contributed to an astonishing development of calligraphy in books as well as in epigraphy. Arabic is written in a cursive script running from right to left, although not all letters can be connected to the left. Naskh, the Arabic script primarily in use today, has rounded forms and emerged in Baghdad during the tenth century. It developed from Kufic script, an older calligraphic form with its straight lines and angles, which was named after the city of Kūfa on the Euphrates. However, in addition to a special Maghrebi script and the Nasta'līq calligraphy style in Iran with its slanted script (from the top right to the bottom left), there is also a variety of decorative forms of epigraphy, for example, "flowering Kufī," whose extended letters can assume leaf and blossom-like forms. These developments, however, all occurred during the Islamic era.

2

Arabia and Islam

Hunting castle Kars al-Heir al-Gharbi near Damascus

From Bertold Spuler, *Age of the Caliphs* (Princeton: Markus Wiener, 1996)

Arabia on the Eve of Islam

There was no comprehensive political order on the Arabian Peninsula prior to the emergence of Islam. The kingdoms of ancient South Arabia were limited to the southwestern corner of the peninsula. The entire region was characterized by a tribal social order; not only the Bedouin herders were organized in tribes, subtribes, and clans, but also the sedentary urban dwellers and farmers. The population of the city of Mecca was comprised of members of the Quraysh tribe, which was in turn divided into a dozen clans, including the powerful Makhzūm and ʻAbd Shams, as well as the less influential Hāshim. The neighboring city of Ṭā'if belonged to the Thaqīf tribe, and five Arab tribes inhabited the Yathrib oasis (later Medina). In pre-Islamic times, the tribes of the Arabian Peninsula were already organized on a genealogical basis predicated on the assumption that all tribes had descended from common ancestors. Qaḥṭān was regarded as the progenitor of the South Arabian tribes, whereas the North Arabian tribes were said to have descended from ʻAdnān. This distinction was evident in a profound antagonism between the two groups that continued to exist far into the Islamic period. Later – we do not know the precise date – the two lines were brought together in a genealogy based on the Old Testament: Qaḥṭān was equated with the Biblical Joktan, a grandson of Noah's son Shem (Genesis 10:25), whereas ʻAdnān was considered a descendant of Ishmael, the outcast son of Abraham and Hagar

(Genesis 16:15). Arabs from South Arabia were regarded (or regarded themselves) as "true, pure Arabs," the *'āriba,* while Arabs from North Arabia were considered *musta'riba,* "arabized Arabs."

Although the various tribes spoke their own dialects, poets had already created a uniform high language that was evidently understood everywhere. The annual fairs served as a means of exchange and also led to a leveling of differences. The locations of the fairs rotated throughout the entire Arabian Peninsula, and periods of a general, binding ceasefire guaranteed that they could be carried out in peace. Important meeting places were also the shrines to different gods and goddesses, such as the Ka'ba, a cube-shaped temple in Mecca dedicated to the god Hubal, and many other places of worship northeast of Mecca, which even today are sites of Islamic pilgrimages (*ḥajj),* of course devoid of such pagan idols.

We know of the world of the Arab gods, at least in broad outlines, through allusions in the Qur'ān and especially through *Kitāb al-Aṣnām (The Book of Idols*) by the Iraqi author Ibn al-Kalbī (737–821). According to the latter, certain tribes controlled the shrines dedicated to particular gods or goddesses, although members of other tribes were also permitted to worship them. The deities appeared as stones or as trees, whose rustling was interpreted as an oracle, and sometimes also as primitive statues of wood or stone. Certain clans were entrusted with caring for the shrines. Hubal, the main god of the Quraysh of Mecca, also appears to have been worshipped under the name *Allāh* (contracted from *al-ilāh,* "deity"). His oracle in the Ka'ba functioned through casting lots with arrows. At his side stood a "goddess," *Allāt,* whose holy district was near the city of Ṭā'if. Manāt, the goddess of fate, was embodied in a black stone on the road from Mecca to Medina, whereas al-'Uzza, the planet Venus, was worshipped in three trees in Nakhla, east of Mecca. The rituals connected with the worship of the god of the Ka'ba and the other shrines in and around Mecca also predate Islam. Stripped of their pagan contexts they were later retained by Muḥammad out of reverence to the Prophet Abraham, Hagar, and their son Ishmael, who were regarded as the shrines' monotheistic founders even in pre-Islamic times.

Pilgrimages and markets, as well as traveling minstrels, provided the first interregional connections among the tribes scattered throughout the Arabian Peninsula. Trade, which was largely concentrated along the Incense Road from Yemen to Syria, that is, from the Indian Ocean to the Mediterranean Sea, also connected the peninsula to the rest of the world. Although Mecca did not lie directly along this route, it was a very active trading city. The Quraysh themselves lived from trade. The annual winter and summer caravans they outfitted (sura 106:2) are mentioned in the Qur'ān and according to Islamic tradition, Muḥammad himself traveled to Syria as a young man.

Judaism and Christianity reached western Arabia in pre-Islamic times both from the north and the south. Roman-Byzantine Syria, whose eastern regions had already been Islamized in antiquity, was Christian. Yemen had been ruled by a Jewish dynasty until a Christian Abyssinian governor took over. In Najrān, there was a strong Christian community led by a bishop; in Yathrib (Medina), three of the five Arab tribes that inhabited the oasis were Jewish.

Virtually nothing is known about how Judaism and Christianity spread in these regions. Contact with these two monotheistic religions, however, left very unambiguous traces in Islam. The Qur'ān is full of stories about Noah and Moses, the ancient patriarchs Abraham, Isaac, Jacob, and Joseph, King David and King Solomon, and the Prophet Jonah, although there are very few direct references to Christianity. While there does not appear to have been either a Jewish or a Christian community in Mecca, Islamic sources do tell of the ḥanīfs, a kind of monotheistic God-seekers without ties to either of the older religions, but no longer satisfied with the faded world of the ancient Arab gods. The Prophet Muḥammad, in other words, emerged in an environment that was by no means unprepared for his message.

The Prophet Muḥammad

Islam is without a doubt a constituting element of the Arab world, at least in the early Islamic period, when the notions of Arab and Muslim largely coincided. According to the Qur'ān, God often says: "These (*letters*) are proofs of this profound scripture. We have revealed it, an Arabic Qur'ān" (sura 12:1–2; see also 41:1 and 43:1). Only the Arab-speaking segment of humanity is addressed in this particular divine revelation, which in another form, by other prophets, and in other languages had already been revealed to other peoples. The Qur'ān "is a scripture that confirms, in Arabic," the mission of other prophets, such as Moses (sura 46:12). The notion that Qur'ānic revelation possessed a universal mission and validity appears to have developed only later.

Born around 570 as a member of the Hāshim clan in the Quraysh tribe in Mecca, Muḥammad was orphaned at an early age and like many Meccans first earned his livelihood as a trader. As an associate and trustee of the wealthy widow Khadīja, he is said to have accompanied a caravan to Syria. There he carried on business, whereupon Khadīja – about fifteen years his senior – married him. After receiving his divine revelation around 610, when he was about 40 years old, he appeared as a prophet (in Arabic *nabī,* similar to the Hebrew *nebi*) of a monotheistic faith that forebode a Judgment Day, thereby vehemently rejecting the ancient polytheistic religions of Arabia. In Mecca, the Prophet was able to gather only a small band of followers. The leading clans in the Quraysh tribe, which feared for their influential position and their income from the pilgrimages to the Ka'ba and other holy shrines in the environs of Mecca, were hostile to Muḥammad and his mission. They harassed his companions and even threatened him. Consequently, in 622 the Prophet and his companions emigrated (*hijra*) to Yathrib (later al-Madīna), about 250 miles northwest of Mecca, referring to themselves as "ones who submit (to God)" (*muslimūn)* and to their faith as "submission" (*islām)* to God's will. The two non-Jewish tribes there had made an agreement with Muḥammad prior to this.

In Yathrib/Medina, the Prophet went from being a persecuted outsider to the powerful leader of an ever-growing community, whose cohesion was guaranteed by the profession of faith in the one God and loyalty to their prophet, rather than by kinship relations and occasional confederacies that existed up to then among Arab tribes. This new community (*umma)* competed with the traditional tribal order of society, although it was not yet in a position to replace it. It was open to all tribes and clans and was also considered indissoluble, as it was traced back to God himself.

During the tens years he was in Medina (622–632), Muḥammad managed to expand the Islamic *umma* virtually throughout the entire Arabian Peninsula. Numerous tribes – both sedentary and nomadic – voluntarily joined the community, which became increasingly powerful. Jews and Arab converts to Judaism living in the oasis of Khaybar in the Ḥijāz mountains agreed contractually to subordinate themselves to the *umma*, as did the Christian community in the bishopric seat of Najrān in northern Yemen. Yemen, which was ruled by the Persians, was won over, as was Muḥammad's hometown Mecca. There, the pagan aristocracy initially fought against the Prophet, with varying results, until the opposing pagan clans of the Quraysh finally decided their future was more secure in the *umma* than in opposition to it. They opened up to the Prophet and converted to Islam in 630. When Muḥammad died two years later, the entire Arabian peninsula was associated with the *umma,* that is, almost all Arabs were united in Islam. This loyalty, however, was tied to Muḥammad personally and was rescinded after his death by some tribes, where their own prophets now appeared. Muḥammad's successor Abü Bakr (632–634) was able again to subjugate the renegades through military force and end the "apostasy" (*ridda*).

The Arab-Islamic Conquests

Only two major kingdoms existed in antiquity and usually opposed each other as rivals: In the west there was the Hellenist world with the later Roman-Byzantine empire, and in the east, the great Persian empire under the Achaemenids, Parthians, and Sassanids. The Islamic *umma* added a third actor to the political stage for the first time. A state emerged where there had previously been none. It quickly began to expand and – similar to the other two – developed into an imperial power.

During the decade in which Muḥammad led the *umma* in Medina, preliminary structures for a state had already been created: the basic features of a system of law that bound the tribes together, a class of administrators sent from Medina, and the rudiments of a system of tributes and taxes. The tribal order of society was not simply abolished as a result, but new "state" structures were superimposed on it.

The political and military elite in the new polity were exclusively Arabs. For this reason, the historian Julius Wellhausen titled his classic description of early Islamic history *The Arab Kingdom and Its Fall* (1927, German 1902). The core of the new elite were Muḥammad's original fellow sufferers and comrades in arms, the first Muslims. The first four caliphs, or "successors" (*khalīfa)*, also came from their ranks: Abū Bakr (632–634), 'Umar (634–644), 'Uthmān (644–656), and 'Alī (656–661), Muḥammad's cousin and son-in-law. All four were members of the Meccan tribe of the Quraysh, who had been distinguished by their religious merit, in particular by their early profession of faith in the new religion (*sābiqa*). All four had also participated in Prophet's hijra, that is, they were "emigrants" (*muhājirūn).* In comparison, the Muslims of Medina, the "helpers" (*anṣār),* receded into the background very early on. None of them became a caliph, although they did at times raise such claims. Rather quickly, however, Mecca's old pagan elite of money and power reasserted its authority even within the Islamic *umma*, pushing out the class of religious meritocrats. The Umayya family, belonging to the Quraysh clan of the 'Abd Shams, assumed the leading role in this. Once a bitter enemy of the Prophet and his mission, they now joined the vanguard in the military expansion of the new state. The Quraysh aristocracy can be seen as one of the driving forces behind the ensuing conquests (*futūḥ,* literally "openings"). Their trade interests had already led them to Syria during the pre-Islamic era. It has been documented that a number of Meccans owned manors in eastern Syria even prior to the conquest. The Umayyad Mu'āwiya, a son of Muḥammad's former adversary Abū Sufyān, played a significant role in conquering Palestine and Syria. As a reward he was appointed governor of Damascus, a position he held for twenty years. His power base was in Syria, and from there he opposed the selection of the fourth caliph 'Alī. After 'Alī was murdered in 661, he was able to claim the title of caliph for himself and establish Damascus as the new capital.

The military expansion of the caliphate began under the second caliph, 'Umar, and quickly led to the conquest of Roman-Byzantine Palestine/Syria and Persian-Sassanid

Mesopotamia (al-'Irāq). In 636, a Byzantine army was defeated at Yarmūk, a left-bank tributary of the Jordan, after which the Byzantine army abandoned Syria. Almost all of the cities of Palestine and Syria surrendered in exchange for more favorable conditions: protection of life and limb, guaranteed property, the continued existence of churches and protection of their property, and the free exercise of religion. In return, the cities paid a tribute, usually in the form of a lump sum. This was later converted into a poll tax (*jizya*) on non-Muslims. According to these treaties, non-Muslims were given the status of "wards" (*dhimmī*). Under these conditions, Damascus surrendered in 635, Jerusalem in 638, Caesarea in Palestine in 640, and Alexandria in 642, bringing all of Egypt under Arab-Islamic rule. The contractual partners of the caliph were the Christian patriarchs and bishops, who were the only remaining public authority once the Byzantine military withdrew.

The decisive battle in Mesopotamia took place against the Persian imperial army around 636 near al-Qādisiyya, west of the lower Euphrates. Directly following this, the Arabs occupied Ctesiphon, residential city of the Great King on the left (eastern) bank of the Tigris (today Salmān Pāk, southeast of Baghdad). Arab Muslims also defeated the Persians in another battle at Nihavend in western Iran in 641 or 642, paving the way for the conquest of the Iranian highlands.

The rapid expansion of the caliphate is an astounding phenomenon that has been explained in various and at times contradictory ways. The most stubborn cliché, although long challenged by historians, is that of zealous masses setting off to conquer the world in order to spread Islam through fire and sword. However, it is difficult if not impossible to reconstruct the motives of actors at the time, as Arabic sources available to us were all compiled from oral tradition long after the events took place. The Qur'ān itself does not express any explicit missionary aims, nor do we have any evidence of a political program of conquest.

Reports about the initial conquests – which are chronologically confusing and uncertain – tell of individual bands of Bedouins who were and had always been active on the borders of the Fertile Crescent and who were encouraged to further endeavors by their momentary successes. The Arab conquests thus appear initially to have remained within the framework of a continuous process in the Fertile Crescent beginning in the third century BCE: the steady and at times wavelike expansion of Semitic-speaking Bedouins from the Syrian Desert – the Akkadians, Canaanites, and Aramaeans. Soon, however, these Arab incursions assumed a completely new dimension and quality, which is apparent in the fact that they expanded far beyond the Fertile Crescent – into Iran, Armenia, and Asia Minor, as well as into Egypt and North Africa. This development can be traced to the imperial desires of the new power center in Medina, although it appeared to have sought only gradually to coordinate the actions of independent armies at the peripheries of the Fertile Crescent. Most of the military leaders came from the Meccan Quraysh and the Medinan helpers *(anṣār),* whereas the rank and file soldiers were predominantly from Bedouin tribes associated with the *umma* who were interested above all in booty. One-fifth of the spoils were traditionally reserved for the caliph, who assumed the role of the pagan tribal sheikh. Later, after state structures had been established, the central government became the recipient and distributor of the regular tax revenues.

The conquests in Palestine and Syria were secured by quartering the individual troop divisions in the larger cities; in Mesopotamia, Egypt, and North Africa, on the other hand, military encampments were set up, which gradually developed into permanent cities: al-Basra in 635, al-Kūfa on the Euphrates in 638, al-Fusṭāṭ (Old Cairo) on the Nile in 641, and al-Qayrawān (Kairouan) in present-day Tunisia in 670. The soldiers *(muqātila)* stationed there were organized according to tribal groups, camping and fighting under their own leaders. They received payment *('atā)* from their regional commander (*amīr*), drawn from spoils and tribute and later from the regular taxes and duties. Like the old religious meritocrats and their descendants, the warriors of the individual tribes also received fixed shares of the endowments entered in an army list or *dīwān* ("list, register" in Persian). The "warriors" – initially only Arabs and Muslims – were thus the beneficiaries of this fiscal system based on taxation of the non-Muslims. The need to subjugate an increasing number of taxpayers to finance a steadily growing Muslim army was certainly one significant motive for the expanding conquests. The capture of the Iranian highlands and central Asia was initiated from the military encampment cities of Basra and Kūfa and continued independently from there. The Maghreb and the Iberian peninsula were taken by armies from Kairouan.

The system described above emerged during the conquests and lasted as long as the conquests continued, into the seventh and eighth centuries, then becoming obsolete.

This was the basis of what Julius Wellhausen referred to as the "Arab Kingdom": the imperial rule of Muslim Arabs over non-Muslim non-Arabs. Nowhere were non-Muslims compelled to convert to Islam; the guarantee of protection *(dhimma)* for non-Muslim subjects became an established part of Islamic divine law *(sharīʿa)*. Mass conversions, after all, would have undermined the financial basis of the dīwān system. It was only gradual change that led to the fall of the "Arab kingdom." Although the religious motive for expanding the Arab empire might be merely one of many, we should not underestimate the role that religion played as the link between the rulers and as the legitimation for their rule. It was not the conversion of the non-believers, but the rule of Muslims over them that was regarded as God's will.

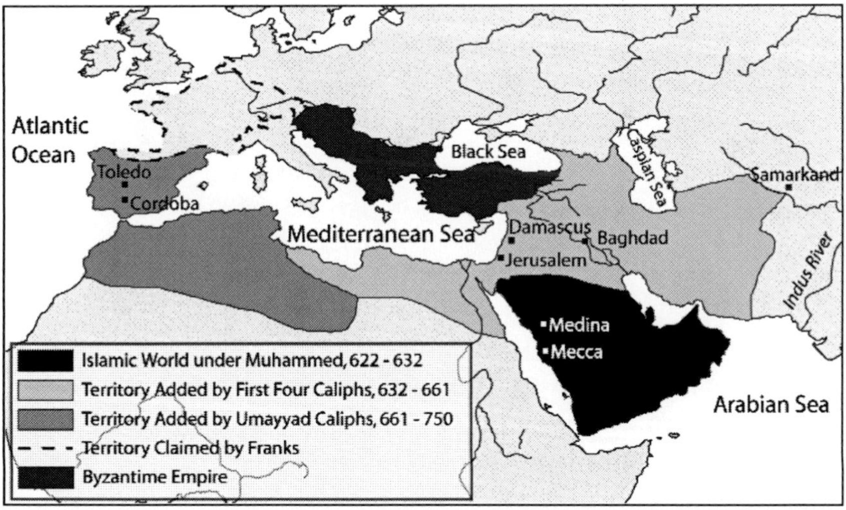

The Spread of Islam, 622–750 CE

From Don and Jean Johnson, *The Human Drama, Vol. II* (Princeton: Markus Wiener, 2006)

The Caliphate of the Umayyads (661–750)

Caliph Mu'āwiya (661–680) was able to ensure the succession of his son Yazīd (680–683) and thus start a dynasty that would rule the Arab empire for ninety years. This marked the definitive establishment of the old aristocracy of the Quraysh in Mecca over the religious meritocracy of young Islam. This rule, however, did not remain unchallenged. In the next generation, descendants of the companions of the Prophet asserted their claims against Yazīd, which led to a bloody intra-Muslim conflict (*fitna,* "strife, trial"). Al-Ḥusayn, son of 'Alī and grandson of the Prophet, was killed in 681 at Kerbela (Karbalā') while trying to incite a rebellion in Iraq. He became the first martyr of the oppositional party of the Sh'ites. The sons of al-Zubayr, a companion of the Prophet, were able to set up a counter-caliphate in Mecca that survived until 691. There continued to be uprisings after this, especially by 'Alid pretenders against the established caliphate.

In the meantime, the Umayyad 'Abd al-Malik (685–705) was able to bring down the Meccan counter-caliphate and reestablish the unity of the empire. He was the most important Umayyad caliph and set in motion a number of significant reforms. Most important was the standardization of administrative language. From that point on, the language used in records and on coins was Arabic instead of Greek, which until that time had been used in the western part of the empire, and Middle Persian (Pahlavi), which had been used in the east. A standardized form of written Arabic was thereby established. The foundation inscription in the interior of the Dome of the Rock in Jerusalem, a glass mosaic frieze, is the oldest extant Arabic monumental inscription. It is at the same time the earliest material evidence of Qur'ān verses. The Dome of the Rock (*Qubbat al-ṣakhra)*, which marks the site of the Prophet Muḥammad's ascension to heaven, bears the foundation date of 691. Its inscription addresses non-Muslims, especially Christians, strongly admonishing them to adopt the strict monotheism of Islam. The meaning of this oldest Islamic monumental construction is disputed. One possible motive was the desire to have something comparable to the splendid Christian Church of the Holy Sepulcher; another might have been the dynasty's wish to demonstrate its own power. 'Abd al-Malik initiated a comprehensive construction program for the project, which was completed by his son and successor al-Walīd I (705–715): The al-Aqsa Mosque (*al-masjid al-aqṣā,* "the farthest mosque," as referred to in the Qur'ān, sura 17:1) was built along the axis of the Dome of the Rock, although it has not survived in its original form. The Umayyad Mosque, which was modeled on this, still exists in Damascus at the site of the Church of St. John, the former Jupiter temple. The buildings of the residence of the Prophet in Medina, in whose inner courtyard he was buried, were replaced by a new, magnificent mosque. The main mosque in al-Fusṭāṭ (Old Cairo) was also rebuilt. With these projects, in which Syrian-Byzantine and Coptic artists played an important role, 'Abd al-Malik and al-Walīd created the seminal examples of Islamic monumental architecture and Islamic architectural decoration.

The conquests continued under the rule of the Umayyads. Although an initial siege of Constantinople (Istanbul) failed in 674–678 and a sea operation against Constantinople in 717–718 was equally unsuccessful due to the Byzantines' use of Greek fire, broad regions in both the west and the east were conquered. In 711, an army of Arabs and Berbers led by Tāriq crossed the Strait of Gibraltar, which henceforth was known as *Jabal Tāriq,* or "Tāriq's Mount," ending the rule of the Visigoths on the Iberian peninsula. At the same time Arab troops advanced into the Indus delta in present-day Pakistan. In present-day Uzbekistan, Bukhara was conquered in 710 and Samarqand in 715. While the Arabs did take the most remote Iranian city, Chach (Tashkent) in 751, this victory ultimately weakened the conquest movement. Even the incursion of a Spanish-Arab force into France, widely discussed in Europe, was brought to a halt between Tours and Poitiers by Charles Martel in 732 and appears in fact to have been nothing more than a foray for spoils, targeting the wealthy St. Martin's Abbey in Tours. In the end, France was not conquered, even though Roussillon and parts of Languedoc and Provence were temporarily subject to Arab rule. The counter-movement by Christian forces to reconquer the Iberian Peninsula (*Reconquista*) already began under Charlemagne.

The final decades of Umayyad rule were characterized for the most part by weak and short-lived caliphates as well as by internal conflicts. The last significant ruler, Hishām (724–743), one of ʿAbd al-Malik's many sons, managed to hold the empire together. Central power was maintained from the Pyrenees to central Asia. The Caspian Gates, the passes at the eastern end of the Caucasian foothills, were fortified against a Turkish invasion from the northern steppes. Like his father and brother, Hishām was also a great builder. Numerous "desert castles" of the Umayyads can be traced back to him; they were used for controlling the Bedouins as well as for the agricultural development of the desert steppes and for hunting lodges. The ruins of Qasr al-Hayr al-Sharqī northeast of Palmyra clearly have the dimensions of a palace city. A wealth of stucco carvings has been preserved from Khirbat al-Mafjar in the Jordan valley, not far from Jericho, including a statue of the caliph (currently kept in the Rockefeller Museum in Jerusalem).

The Umayyads maintained their domestic rule through alternating support from northern and southern Arabian tribes. The Islamic *umma* had never been able to overcome the regional differences. The "Arab empire" ultimately fell, in part because it was unable to integrate the growing circles of people who wanted to be part of the *umma.* Islam claims to be egalitarian: All Muslims are said to be equal before God. In reality, however, not only did older tribal structures with their particular loyalty relationships remain intact, but new groups that joined the *umma* had difficulty asserting themselves over the established elites. In addition to the Meccan emigrants *(muhājirūn)*, there were the Medinan "helpers" *(anṣār),* followed by the Meccans who had retained their pagan beliefs to the end and the Arab Bedouin tribes that had been won over or subjugated and then integrated into the *umma.* And finally there was a growing number of converted non-Arab Muslims, who had a client relationship with the ruling Arab elites and were therefore called *mawālī* ("clients"). The dehgans, the Persian knightly nobility, quickly converted to Islam almost en masse, bringing their vassals and tenant farmers with them. As auxiliary military troops and as local authorities and tax collectors, they were indispensable to the Arabs and were thus allowed to retain their old privileges, although the Arab aristocracy refused to grant them equal status.

Arab tribal units in dispute with the central government over the distribution of spoils and tax revenues incited a rebellion, in alliance with the Iranian *mawālī*, which started in the most remote northeast corner of Iran in 747 and ended in 750 with the conquest of Iraq and the taking of Damascus. This opposition was also backed by Sh'ite groups, who regarded the Umayyads as parvenus and believed that the ''Alids, the descendents of Muḥammad's cousin and brother-in-law 'Alī, were the sole legitimate successors to the Prophet. Later Arab historiography has accused the Umayyads of lacking religious legitimacy, claiming that they debased the caliphate into a secular kingdom (*mulk*), although this is a religiously colored judgment that historians need not accept. The caliphate of the Umayyads of Damascus was one of the most splendid epochs in Arab history. Court literature and monumental architecture reached an apex and the political power of the Umayyad caliphate, which reached from southern France to the Indus, was never again achieved. The fall of the dynasty brought the dissolution of the caliphate only 120 years after the death of Muḥammad.

The ʻAbbāsid Caliphate of Baghdad

With the fall of the Umayyads in 750, which is referred to as the "ʻAbbāsid revolution," a dynasty came to power that would occupy the caliphate for more than half a millennium, until the Mongol invasion of 1258. The ʻAbbāsids were the descendants of ʻAbbās, an uncle of Muḥammad, and were thus closely related to the Prophet – in contrast to the Umayyads. Muḥammad's direct blood descendants, the ʻAlids, who initially supported the overthrow of the Umayyads, were again left empty-handed. Their supporters, the "party" (*Shīʻa)*, now became a fixed part of the opposition.

The revolutionary army that had brought down the old regime through its march from central Asia to Iraq and on to Syria and Egypt was comprised primarily of discontented Arabs. Although the new dynasty was Arab and Qurayshi, like its predecessor, the exclusivity of the "Arab empire" could never be reestablished. Persian "clients" had played a significant role in the coup, and men from their ranks began assuming important positions in the army, administration, royal court, and in spiritual life. A geographical shift, which included the establishment of a new capital, accelerated this process. The new rulers remained in Iraq and, after some consideration, decided to establish a new imperial residence and palace city near the old town of Baghdād on the west bank of the Tigris, calling it Madīnat al-Salām, the "City of Peace." Al-Manṣūr (754–775) was the second ‘Abbāsid caliph. Around 758 he started building a circular grounds based on a Persian model, with a palace and mosque in the center. At the perimeter, inside the surrounding wall, there were government offices (dīwāns) and residences for officials and functionaries. The army was quartered outside the city. The Round City of Manṣūr, which has disappeared without a trace, was completed in 762. Markets soon developed at the four arterial roads leading out of the city. These grew into suburbs, so that the palace facility quickly expanded into an actual city. The caliph and his successor also built a number of castles on both banks of the Tigris in 773, which served as residences instead of the Round City. Under Caliph Hārūn al-Rashīd (786–809) and his son al-Ma’mūn (813–833), the metropolis encompassed a densely populated area of almost four square miles with an estimated population of almost one million. It was the largest and most populous city in the world at the time.

Around this time, changes became evident in the court of the Baghdad caliphs. While the Umayyads in Damascus and in their desert castles acted like powerful Arab tribal sheikhs, the ceremonies of the ‘Abbāsids in Baghdad increasingly assumed the splendor of Great Kings in Middle-Eastern antiquity. Hidden away in his Round City far from the masses, the caliph had contact only with privileged people. Like the Sassanid Persian king and the Byzantine emperor, he held audiences concealed behind a curtain, his rank emphasized by his crown or diadem (*tāj*), a crown that hung over his head by a chain (*shamsa*), or other precious insignias. In addition to their first names, caliphs assumed an epithet when they were crowned, such as al-Mansūr (the

Victorious), al-Rashīd (the Upright), and al-Ma'mūn (the Trustworthy). A special feature of 'Abbāsid rule was the emergence of the office of the vizier (*wazīr* = "helper"), who served as a kind of chief administrator, controlling and coordinating the major government ministries (dīwāns) – taxes, army, and chancellery – and directing domestic and foreign policies. Even before the office had been firmly established, the Iranian Barmakid family from the area of present-day Afghanistan – Yaḥyā ibn Khālid and his sons al-Faḍl and Ja'far – exercised almost unlimited power in Baghdad during the first seventeen years in Hārūn's reign, until the caliph forcibly removed them in 803.

The caliphate began to shrink after the 'Abbāsid Revolution. Once Islamic rule became rooted in the provinces, the differences between provincial interests and those of the central government became increasingly apparent. The extremely long distances made communication, and thus direct administrative control of the peripheries, difficult. Baghdad was no longer able to support the armies necessary to hold together the huge empire between the Pyrenees and the Indus.

Rule was regionalized according to two models. The first was the establishment of states independent of Baghdad. Arab warriors on the Pyrenean peninsula refused to recognize the new dynasty. In 736 they took in a fugitive Umayyad prince who had escaped the massacre of his family and who was able to establish himself as the "commander" (*amīr*) of al-Andalus – that is, the Islamic Pyrenean peninsula – and pass on his rule to his descendants. In present-day Morocco another refugee, Idrīs, a descendant of the Prophet, was able to gain the support of the Awrāba.

This Berber tribe had occupied the Roman city of Volubilis and helped Idrīs to power. Fez (Fās), founded by Idrīs in 789, was expanded in 808 by his son Idrīs II. Other Arab refugees from Andalusia and Kairouan made the city into the first Arab settlement in the midst of the Berber tribes of the western Maghreb.

The other model was practiced in Kairouan starting in 800. This Arab garrison town in present-day Tunisia was occupied in 761 by an ʻAbbāsid army and made a subject of Baghdad. Caliph Hārūn al-Rashīd installed Ibn al-Aghlab, an officer in this army, as a governor and military commander (*amīr*) in 800. He founded a *de facto* independent gubernatorial dynasty, the Aghlabids (800–909). With the approval of the caliph, who remained the nominally recognized commander in chief, Ibn al-Aghlab governed over the central Maghreb and Sicily, which was conquered between 827 and 878. The emir paid the caliph an annual tribute and, as a sign of the caliph's supremacy, agreed that he be named at the invocation to close Friday sermons (*khuṭba*) and on coins (*sikka*). Similar dynasties headed by governors nominally subject to Baghdad were later established in Egypt as well as in eastern Iran and central Asia, greatly limiting the actual power of the caliphs in Baghdad. The conquests came to a halt and, despite numerous campaigns, Byzantine Asia Minor could not be conquered in the name of Islam.

Al-ʻArabiyya: High Arabic Language and Literature

Baghdad bookseller Ibn al-Nadīm compiled a "catalog" (*fihrist*) in 988, indexing all the authors he knew and their works. He reported that more than one hundred shops of book scribes and booksellers could be found on a single lane of the bazaar in the capital of the caliphate and that he knew of a Baghdad bibliophile who hoarded the manuscripts of six generations of learned authors in a chest: on parchment, Egyptian papyrus, Chinese paper, and leather scrolls, all of which had been marked with the name of the author and certified. Ibn al-Nadīm listed more than six thousand book titles in his "catalog," which was by no means limited to Muslim authors. He was particularly interested in Greek philosophers.

The Islamic conquests not only expanded the horizons of the Arabs immensely, but also provided them with access to new technologies. Following a battle between Arab troops and Chinese border guards at the River Talas (in present-day Kyrgyzstan near the border to Kazakhstan) in 751, it was discovered that several paper producers were among the Chinese prisoners of war, who had been settled in Samarqand. Paper production soon became a local industry in eastern Iran and was brought to Baghdad by al-Faḍl, a Barmakid, in 794, quickly spreading westward from there. Paper was one of the prerequisites for the incredible production of Arabic literature that began in the ninth and tenth centuries. Another was the existence of the metropolis of Baghdad and the court of the caliph, which served not only as a crossroads and gathering point for influences from the four corners of the known world, but also as a place where science and literature were valued and promoted.

Arabic literature of the ʻAbbāsid period developed above all from religious writings. An unprecedented amount of information, which until that time had been passed down primarily in oral form, was collected and put down in writing. During the final years of the Umayyad period, Ibn Isḥāq (died ca. 767) of Medina had already compiled the hagiography (*sīra*) of the Prophet Muḥammad. His work has survived in an abridged edition by Ibn Hishām of Basra (died ca. 830). Al-Wāqidī (747–823), a protĕgĕ of Caliph Hārūn al-Rashīd and the Barmakid Yaḥyā, collected the chronicles of Muḥammad's military expeditions and campaigns (*al-maghāzī*). His secretary Ibn Saʻd (784–845) compiled the biographies of the Prophet and his companions, as well as those of the most important personalities of subsequent generations, into what is today a nine-volume work. All of these authors were "clients," *mawālī*, that is, non-Arab Muslims. Ibn al-Kalbī of Kūfa (737–821), whose *Book of Idols* includes extensive information about ancient Arab gods and their shrines and rites, lived in Baghdad for a time under the caliph al-Mahdī (775–785).

Kitāb al-kharāj, a treatise on taxation written for Caliph Hārūn al-Rashīd by Abū Yūsuf (died in 798), a Baghdad judge, marks the beginning of Arabic legal writings. Abū Yūsuf was a student of the great Iraqi legal scholar Abū Hanīfa of Kūfa (died in 767), whose mausoleum in Baghdad remains a Sunnī pilgrimage site to the present day. The

Sunnī legal schools (singular *madhhab*), which continue to exist even today, emerged from the student circles of Abū Hanīfa, the Medinan Mālik (died in 796), the Palestinian al-Shāfi'ī (767–820), who died in Egypt, and Ibn Ḥanbal (780–855) of Baghdad and were a prerequisite for the flourishing, extensive production of Islamic legal writings, which today fill entire libraries with their fundamental treatises, commentaries, and supercommentaries.

A short time later the traditionaries also started their collections. At first they compiled the oral traditions, usually short, anecdotal reports about the sayings and decisions of the Prophet Muḥammad, which had become increasingly important in legal, theological, and political debate beginning around 700. They reviewed the sayings according to a criteria of authenticity they themselves had developed and recorded them systematically in written form. The most notable collector of these traditions, or *Hadīth* ("events"), was al-Bukhārī (810–870), a scholar of Persian descent from central Asia, who traveled to Baghdad, Mecca, and Egypt "in search of knowledge" (*fī talab al-'ilm*). The Sunnīs regard his *Saḥīḥ* ("The Authentic"), containing 2762 hadiths, as the most important religious work after the Qur'ān. The other five Sunnī standard collections of the Prophet's traditions from this era emerged in a similar way, by means of extended travels in order to collect such materials. By and large they were written in Arabic by Iranian or central Asian men. In addition to the Qur'ān and its commentaries, it was primarily these collections of traditions and legal works that allowed classical High Arabic to spread to the remotest corners of the caliphate after having been standardized in Basra and Baghdad.

This growing interest in the history and early period of

Islam helped to strengthen the sense of cohesion among Muslims, whether they were of Arab descent or not. The first recountings of historical events occurred orally in the form of individual tidings (*khabar*), which were then recorded during the 'Abbāsid period in written form in chronological collections, as was done for the sayings of the Prophet as well. The oldest preserved chronicle is one by Khalīfa ibn Khayyāt (died in 854), a Basran. The history of the Arab-Islamic conquests was compiled in Baghdad by al-Balādhurī (died in 892), a man of Persian descent. The zenith of early 'Abbāsid historiography is *Ta'rikh al-rusul wa al-muluk* (*The History of Prophets and Kings)*, a chronicle of the world from creation to the author's present, written by the Iranian Ṭabarī (839–923). This mammoth, thirteen-volume work follows his travels to Syria and Egypt using older collections in Baghdad, providing most of our knowledge about early Islamic history.

In addition to these works related to Islam, the belles lettres also developed. This genre was unambiguously secular in nature and was written and read not by the religious scholars (*'ulamā'*), but by the courtiers and officials of the dīwāns, the "secretaries" (*kuttāb*). The apex of courtly poetry can be found in the poems of Abū Nuwās (died in 815), a Persian "client" at the court of Hārūn al-Rashīd and his son al-Amīn, who despite his Persian background was and continues to be celebrated by Arabs as one of their greatest poets, although his verses, which rebound in wine, women, and song, certainly have not found the approval of pious religious scholars. The most significant writer of entertaining secular prose (*adab)* which was often based on translations from Middle Persian is al-Jāḥiẓ (776–869), a member of a "client" family from Basra. His satires and *Kitāb al-bukhalā'* (published in English as both *The Book of Misers* and *Avarice and the Avaricious*), his polemics and his encyclopedias, such as *Kitāb al-ḥayawān* (*The Book of Animals*), remain peerless examples of Arab prose even today. Finally, it was during the era of Hārūn al-Rashīd and the Barmakids in Baghdad that the oldest Arabic core of *1001 Nights* was written.

This rich literary life gave rise to High Arabic, or *'Arabiyya,* as Arabic grammar is also a product of 'Abbāsid Iraq. The first important Arab grammarians and lexicographers, Sībawayh (died 786) and al-Khalīl (died 791), lived and worked in Basra. Although this interest in grammar originally arose from a religious desire to understand enigmatic passages in the Qur'ān as precisely as possible, a purely scholarly interest in the subject quickly developed as well. The Basra school, in contrast to the Kūfa school, attached great importance to standardizing the language, seeking to adapt the rules of the proper, high language, or *fusḥa* ("most eloquent, purest"), to the Bedouins' exemplary use of language, which was considered especially pure. Classical *'Arabiyya,* the high language, emerged between the eighth and tenth centuries in Iraq from the mutual influences of spoken language, literature, and standardized grammar. Even today it continues to unite all Arabs.

The Arab Reception of Antiquity

High Arabic, which assumed its standardized form in Baghdad and Basra, was also understood by educated classes in Samarqand and Bukhara, in Cordoba and Toledo, regardless of whether they were of Arab descent or not. ʻArabiyya offered a means of communication that was used from the Chinese border to the marches of France, facilitating a cultural exchange that the world had seen only once before, during the Hellenist age. Arabic now took the place of Greek, as Islam replaced Hellenism. Although Arabs were able to conquer neither Asia Minor nor Constantinople and Greece, three of the most important Hellenist metropolises did come under their control: Seleukeia on the Tigris, Antiocheia (Antioch), and Alexandria. Alexandria no longer had the central role in science that it had occupied well into the fifth century, but the heritage of antiquity was still very much alive throughout the eastern Mediterranean realm, and it was eagerly appropriated by Arabs. The story that the second caliph, ʻUmar, destroyed the library of Alexandria is merely a legend.

According to tradition, the Caliph al-Ma'mūn (813–833) reported that Aristotle once appeared to him in a dream: "A man with light, reddish skin, a high forehead, thick eyebrows, a bald head, dark blue eyes, and handsome features was sitting at a lectern." The caliph turned to the great scholar and questioned him. Encouraged by this encounter, he then began collecting Greek manuscripts and having them translated into Arabic. This legend is a symbolic representation of an actual process that continued over several generations. Aramaic-speaking Christians – who comprised the vast majority of the caliph's subjects in the Fertile Crescent – were particularly responsible for the survival and transmission of the heritage of antiquity. Much of Greek literature had already been translated into Aramaic, and translations into Arabic were usually completed through this intermediate step. The first known translator into Arabic was a Christian, Yaḥyā (Yuḥannā) al-Bitrīq ("Patrikios"), who translated numerous medical works as well as Ptolemy's *Tetrabiblos,* purportedly commissioned by Caliph al-Manṣūr (754–775). His son, who was also named Yaḥyā, converted to Islam and was the protĕgĕ of a vizier of the caliph al-Ma'mūn. The younger Yaḥyā started translating the works of Aristotle: *On Heavens, Meteorology, History of Animals, Politics,* and the basic work on logic, the *Organon.* He also translated Plato's *Timaeus,* which investigates the nature of the physical world.

In 830, al-Ma'mūn opened his famous *Bayt al-ḥikma,* the House of Wisdom, which was not a university, as is sometimes claimed, but a library hall, whose constantly growing inventory of manuscripts was accessible to scholars. The caliph also sponsored translations into Arabic. A Syrian Christian, Yūḥannā ibn Māsawayh, was the first director of this institute. He was succeeded by Ḥunayn ibn Isḥāq (Latinized as Johannitius), son of a Christian apothecary from al-Ḥīra, the ancient capital of the Lakhmids on the Euphrates. He is said to have learned Greek in Alexandria and improved his Arabic in Basra. As a young doctor he entered into service for al-Ma'mūn and remained active under Caliph al-Mutawakkil (847–861). Ḥunayn is the most important translator of the Baghdad School. He translated from Greek primarily into his native Aramaic, and less often into Arabic. He is responsible for the Arabic translation of numerous treatises of Galen and other ancient physicians such as Hippocrates, Rufus of Ephesus, and Paul of Aegina. He also translated works of the pharmacologist Discorides, the geographer and astronomer Ptolemy, the mathematician Archimedes, and Plato and the Neoplatonists Porphyrios and Alexander of Aphrodisias. Ḥunayn died in 873, but the Baghdad school of translation continued into the tenth century, supported by caliphs, viziers, and other high-ranking officials. In 991 or 993, Shapur ibn Ardashir, the Persian vizier of Caliph al-Rādī, founded a House of Knowledge *(dār al-'ilm)* in the Baghdad suburb of al-Karkh. It contained a library with more than ten thousand volumes and was also open to foreign scholars staying in Baghdad.

Arab interest in Greek texts was selective. Only works of prose were translated, in particular those dealing with scientific or philosophical subjects. Literature – epics, drama, and lyric poetry – was completely absent. Most of Plato's dialogues remained untranslated as well. Aristotle, in contrast, was regarded as "the philosopher" par excellence; and everything that came after him – especially the extensive works of Plotinus and the Neoplatonists – was associated with him. The Greek words *philosophos* and *philosophia* were borrowed in Arabic as *faylasūf* and *falsafa*, as were countless terms from the fields of medicine, botany, pharmacology, and astronomy.

The significance of the Arab reception of antiquity is twofold. In the first place, it enriched and expanded intellectual life in the Islamic world. On this basis, a philosophy arose that was independent and Arabic – albeit only "Islamic" to a limited extent. Its first representative was al-Kindī (ca. 800–870), the descendant of an Arab family from Kūfa, who was a protĕgĕ of the caliphs al-Ma'mūn and al-Mu'taṣim (833–842) and a teacher to one of the latter's sons. Kindī's system was greatly influenced by Aristotelian and Neoplatonist thought. The philosopher al-Fārābī (872–950), a Turk from Transoxania, also resided in Baghdad and later in Syria. The physician and philosopher Ibn Sīnā (Latinized as Avicenna, 980–1037) was born in Bukhara and lived and taught in many cities in Iran. His central texts, *Al-Qānūn (The Canon of Medicine)* and the philosophical *Kitāb al-Shifā' (The Book of Healing),* came to be standard works, not only among Arabs, but soon in the Christian western world as well. The religious scholars (*'ulamā)* of Islam always suspected that Greek philosophy was heretical, although they often employed Aristotelian logic in theological disputes. The natural sciences, on the other hand, were adopted without reservation and developed further. The "ancient sciences" (*al-'ulūm al-qadīma*) were added to the canon of the religious – that is, Islamic – sciences as a matter of course.

The Arab reception of antiquity, however, proved to be as important for the Christian Western world as it was for the Arabs themselves. While monastery libraries did contain Latin texts, Greek literature existed at most in Latin translation. The mediating role played by the Arabs here was invaluable. Texts from antiquity translated into Arabic found their way to western Europe, above all via the Iberian peninsula. After Charlemagne took Barcelona in 801, the creation of the Spanish March (Marcia Hispănica) in Catalonia brought the Franks in close contact with the "Saracens," as Christians called Muslim Arabs. The name comes from the Greek term *Sarakenoi*, an Arab tribe on the Sinai Peninsula. Gerbert d'Aurillac, a scholar and cleric who later became Pope Silvester II (999–1003), spent three years in his youth studying in the Catalonian bishopric of Vic and in the nearby Ripoll monastery. There he used Arabic sources to develop his knowledge of mathematics and astronomy, using primarily astronomical instruments such as the astrolabe and the armillary sphere. The Christian reconquest of Toledo in 1085 by King Alphonse VI of Castile created another site where Europeans encountered Arabic literature. The circle of Archbishop Raimund I (1126–1151) was responsible for extensive translations from Arabic into Latin, performed by learned clerics from all over Europe. In addition to Michael Scot and Robert of Ketton (Robertus Ketenensis), Herman of Carinthia, also known as Herman Dalmatin, worked there as well. Peter the Venerable, the abbot of Cluny, encouraged Robert to prepare the first Latin translation of the Qur'ān, a project that was completed in 1143. While the conquest of Jerusalem during the first crusade in 1099 had sparked interest in Islam, scholarly interest independent of the church's missionary aims emerged quickly. Aside from the Qur'ān, Robert also translated Al-Khwārizmī's *Algebra* into Latin in 1145. Central among those works of antiquity that reached the Christian Western world through Islamic Spain were those dealing with mathematics and astronomy. Arab-

Islamic scholars also produced independent contributions of their own, such as the astronomical tables of the Spaniard Maslama al-Majrīṭī ("of Madrid," died ca. 1007), which were rendered into Latin in 1126 by English scholar and cleric Adelard of Bath. About fourteen years later, the tables of the elder al-Battānī (Albategnius), which were based on observations made in Mesopotamia around 900, were translated by Plato of Tivoli. Gerhard of Cremona translated the *Toledan Tables,* which are based on observations by many Muslim and Jewish astronomers of Spain, including al-Zarqālī (Arzachel). Copernicus cited Albategnius and Arzachel in his major work *De revolutionibus orbium coelestium (On the Revolutions of the Heavenly Spheres),* focusing on their corrections of Ptolemy.

The Andalusian Aristotelian Ibn Rushd (Latinized as Averroēs, 1126–1198) of Cordoba exercised perhaps the greatest influence on Western philosophy. After his extensive oeuvre was translated into Latin, it triggered a wave of Aristotelianism throughout Western Europe. It was in fact through Averroēs that the Western world was introduced to Aristotle, and even Thomas Aquinas was forced to critically address the Latin Averroism.

Arabic Numerals and the Zero

During his studies in Vic and Ripoll in Catalonia from roughly 967 to 991, Gerbert d'Aurillac, later Pope Silvester II, was one of the first Western scholars to become familiar with "Arabic" numerals and how to do arithmetic with them. The Romans, in contrast to the Greeks, had also used a numerical system, but it was poorly suited for arithmetic computation. The Arabs, on the other hand, had a much more practical and versatile tool for writing numbers, composed only of glyphs for the digits one to nine and the zero. It is the same system – except for a few graphic modifications, in particular a ninety-degree rotation – that continues to be used throughout the world today as "Arabic numerals." The Arabs themselves referred to this method of numerical computation as "Indian arithmetic," which suggests that they presumed the system originated in India. What was unique about this system was the use of decimal positions and the related use of a special sign as a placeholder, the zero – *ṣifr* in Arabic, "empty" – which corresponds to the words *cipher* or *zero*. The Sumerians and Babylonians also used a decimal place value system and eventually even developed a sign for zero, but their system was never popularized. The Indian system had probably already spread to Iran during the late Sassanid dynasty. In India itself, the astronomer Aryabhata (ca. 476) had worked with nine ciphers, and the mathematician Brahmagupta

(598–665) had developed arithmetic rules that used a zero. The Iranian Muḥammad al-Khwārizmī (from Khwārizm, the inland delta of the Oxus/Amu Darya, south of the Aral Sea) is responsible for the general widespread use of the system. In 820 he wrote his fundamental work *Al-Khwarizmi on the Hindu Art of Reckoning*, which describes the basic arithmetic operations and setting up of equations. The treatise introduced the system and thus made it practicable throughout the Arab world. The work became known in the West in its Latin translation as *De numero Indorum* and in an adapted form as *Liber Algorismi de pratica arismetrice*. The Latinized form of Khwārizmī is *Algorismus,* which led to the coining of the mathematical term "algorithm." Another work by Khwārizmī was even more significant: *al-Mukhtaṣar fī ḥisāb al-jabr wal-muqābala* (*The Compendious Book on Calculation by Completion and Balancing*). *Al-gabr* or *al-jabr* – literally the "setting" of a dislocated bone – actually refers to the completion or transposition of terms from one side of an equation to the other, whereas "balancing" refers to what we normally call "reduction." When Robert of Chester (Robertus Castrensis) translated this work in 1145 under the Latin title *Liber algebras et almucabola* and a short time later Gerhard of Cremona prepared an improved translation entitled *De jebra et al-mucabola,* the way was paved not only for "Hindu reckoning" in the West, but also the term for it: algebra.

Arabization and Islamization

The caliphate established the framework for two related but clearly distinct processes: linguistic Arabization and religious Islamization, which did go hand in hand with one another, but occurred at different tempos and with varied success in the various countries. Neither process was ever definitively concluded.

Arabic, the language of the Qur'ān and thus of divine revelation, became the language of all religious and juristic writings. Under Caliph 'Abd al-Malik (685–705) it became the sole official language; under the 'Abbāsid caliph of Baghdad it was also established as the language of scholarship, spoken by scholars and the educated from Samarqand to Toledo and from the Caucasus to Yemen. In addition, during the conquest period the Arab army had carried their language to distant garrisons, where it initially existed in scattered linguistic enclaves, such as Old Cairo in Egypt or Kairouan in present-day Tunisia, isolated from the surrounding indigenous language environments.

On the Arabian Peninsula, the North Arabic of the Ḥijāz rapidly replaced Old South Arabic. North Arabic, which is now generally referred to simply as Arabic, is also spoken in Yemen today. Old South Arabic has survived only in small communities there: Mehri on the mainland and Soqotri on the island of Socotra in the Indian Ocean. Both of these languages have preserved the grammatical structures of Old South Arabic, but their vocabularies are now North Arabic to a great degree.

Within the Fertile Crescent, Arabic eclipsed Aramaic, which had been the local language since about 1000 BCE, spoken by all groups in the population regardless of their religious faith. It showed particular resistance to change as the language of the literature and liturgy of the Christian churches – the Syrian Jacobite as well as the Nestorian Church in the former Persian empire. Aramaic is spoken even today by Christians in Syria in the area around Ma'lūlū north of Damascus and among the "Assyrian" or "Chaldean" (Nestorian) Christians in the border triangle of Syria, Iraq, and Turkey.

Iran, on the other hand, resisted Arabization. Although there as well, Arabic was the language of Islamic literature, philosophy, and science, the Semitic language, which is starkly distinct from Indo-Germanic Middle Persian, was never adopted by the Iranian populace. Although powerful Arabic-speaking colonies were established in the aftermath of the conquest, (New) Persian nevertheless became the national language of literature beginning in the tenth century, initially for lyric and epic poetry, and soon afterward for secular prose as well. Vizier al-Bal'amī produced a Persian translation and edited version of Ṭabarī's great chronicle of the world in 963, and around 995 Ferdowsi wrote the *Shāh-nāmeh (Book of Kings)*, which became the Persian national epic. Ibn Sīnā (Avicenna) also wrote scientific prose in Persian and verse in both Arabic and Persian. In preserving its national language and traditions, Iran remained outside of the Arab world.

In Egypt, the use of Arabic was long limited to the al-

Fusṭāṭ (Old Cairo) military camp and a number of garrisons such as Alexandria or Aswān, whereas in rural regions the old languages of the pharaohs were spoken in their most modern form, Coptic (Arabic *qifṭī* or *qubṭī,* meaning "Egyptian"), and maintained as the language of literature and liturgy of the Coptic church. Because Arabic, rather than Greek, was introduced as the official, administrative language and was the only language the authorities permitted, it soon became the spoken language as well, especially among the educated classes. Today Egypt is an Arab country; Coptic is used only in church liturgy and is no longer understood even by Christians.

Libya and the Maghreb comprised the Latin, western part of the Roman Empire. Latin was the language of the urban populace and the Catholic Church. Large segments of the population, peasants and Bedouins alike, however, spoke those languages referred to jointly as "Berber" – literally, "barbarous." There had been a steady decline in the number of Roman cities in North Africa since the third century, causing the Latin-speaking urban population to diminish. Consequently, the Arabs encountered only moderately urbanized landscapes when they conquered the region at the end of the seventh century. Here, too, al-Qayrawān (Kairouan), the military settlement from the period of conquest, and smaller urban garrisons were the locus of Arabization. While the military was continually supplemented and reinforced with advancing troops, the rural population remained Berber and retained their own languages. The first major immigration of entire Bedouin clans and tribes did not occur before 1050, when the government in Cairo took the tribal branches of the Hilāl, Sulaym, and Ma'qil, who had become nomadic in Upper Egypt east of the Nile, relocated them across the river, and unleashed them on the apostate Maghreb. In 1052 the Bedouin armies defeated the emir of Kairouan at Jabal Haydarān in southern Tunisia and, as a contemporary chronicler noted, inundated the entire country "like a swarm of locusts." This marked the beginning of an unremitting flow of immigrant Arab Bedouins into the Maghreb, as the various tribes and clans followed their relatives from the Sinai and the Arabian Peninsula. The actual extent of Bedouin devastation in the former Roman *Africa, Numidia, and Mauritania* is disputed among scholars. While the immigrating Arab tribes destroyed neither cities nor roads and bridges, their advance resulted in the unambiguous displacement of Berber nomads, especially the Zenāta tribe, from Algeria's high plateau, which became grazing areas for Arab Bedouins. The Berbers were forced into the mountains, where they continue to live today as farmers and seminomads. Whereas only remnants of Berber-speaking peoples can still be found in Libya and Tunisia, the Kabyles (from Arabic *qabīla,* "tribe") in Algeria make up thirty percent of the population. The westernmost region of present-day Morocco was the least Arabized; here the Berber-speaking population survived primarily in the high mountains of the Atlas range and the Rif, where they comprise about forty percent of the population today. The Bedouin invasion reached as far south as Mauritania. The Arabic dialects of the Maghreb are those of the immigrant Bedouins.

The Iberian Peninsula remained largely Latin-speaking, even under Islamic rule. Only a segment of the immigrants were Arabs; over the course of the centuries, Berbers made up a much larger proportion. Nevertheless, *al-Andalus,* as the entire peninsula was called (presumably a Visigothic word), was part of the Arab world. The southern half of the peninsula was most strongly influenced by the foreign religion, culture, and language, due in part to the Christian *Reconquista* advancing from the north. Whereas Barcelona returned to Christian rule as early as 801, Toledo in 1085, and Zaragoza in 1118, Cordoba remained Islamic until 1236, Sevilla until 1248, and Granada until 1492. The linguistic influence on Spanish (Castilian) can be recognized even today in the numerous borrowings from Arabic. While the rivers in the north have retained their ancient names: Ebro, Duero/Douro, and Tajo/Tejo, those in the south have Arabic roots, as is evident in their compounding with the word *al-wādī:* Guadalupe, Guadiana, Guadalete, Guadalquivir (*al-Wādi al-kabīr,* "the great river").

Sicily *(Siqilliya)* was part of the Arab world for a much shorter length of time. The Tunisian Aghlabids' conquest of the Byzantine island lasted from 827 to 878. Palermo (*Bālarm*), the seat of the Arab emir, was called *al-Madīna* ("the city"); Taormia became *al-Mu'izziyya.* Numerous locations have retained their old Arabic names, such as Marsala (*Marsā 'Alī*) and Caltabellotta (*Qal'at al-ballūṭ,* "fortress of the oak"). Even the Arabic name for Mount Etna, *al-Jebel* ("the mountain"), has been incorporated into the local name for the mountain, Mongibello. Linguistically the island appears to have been largely Arabized. In any case, Greek disappeared entirely when the island was re-Christianized and then completely Latinized following the Norman conquest (1060–1091).

The process of religious Islamization should be distinguished from that of linguistic Arabization. Although the two were parallel developments, there are important distinctions between them.

In Iran and Iraq, the Zoroastrian "state church" of the Sassanids perished with the fall of the Persian empire. The fire temples were destroyed or fell into ruin. This development was probably the result of the rapid conversion to Islam by the dehgans, the Persian knightly nobility. When almost the entire aristocracy converted en masse to the new religion, the rest of the populace followed. It is certainly significant that – in contrast to the Christian churches – the priestly hierarchy here simply ceased to exist. The "magicians" *(majūs),* as the Arabs referred to the Zoroastrians, were able to enjoy the status of *dhimmīs,* since they were monotheists and considered "People of the Book," as were Christians and Jews. A large portion of Zoroastrian scripture was not codified until the early Islamic period, especially under the 'Abbāsid caliphs. All of this, however, did not prevent the almost complete disappearance of Zoroastrianism. Only small communities have survived to the present, primarily in central and eastern Iran. There is also a Parsi (i.e., Persian) minority on the Indian subcontinent.

In contrast, the Nestorian church, which was officially recognized in the Persian empire, continued under caliphate rule. The primate of the church, the Catholicos, established his seat in the newly founded city of Baghdad, playing an important role at the court of the caliph as the officially recognized head of his church. Remnants of the Nestorian church, which calls itself the "Assyrian" or "Chaldean" church, are present today especially in northern Iraq and across the borders to Turkey and Iran. There are numerous Christian churches in Mosul on the Tigris, which is the seat of both a Jacobite bishop, or maphrian, and the Chaldean (Nestorian) metropolitan. The Jews, who had been residents of the country since the Babylonian captivity (597 or 586 BCE), were of course also "People of the Book." The Babylonian Talmud originated here. During the Sassanid dynasty the seat of the Jewish exilarch or "head of the exile" (Arabic *Ra's al-jālūt*), from the lineage of David, was in Ctesiphon. The exilarch later resided in Baghdad, where – like the Nestorian Catholicos – he was an esteemed member of the caliph's court.

In contrast, followers of the religion founded by Mani (215–277), which started in Iraq, were persecuted and systematically murdered by Muslims. The Manichaeans were dualists and therefore were regarded with suspicion by the strictly monotheistic Muslims. The severe persecution by the 'Abbāsid caliphs between 780 and 795 destroyed Manichaeism. The seat of their leader – originally in Babylon – was moved in the late tenth century to Samarqand, where many Manichaeans had immigrated. Manichaeans are known to have still been living in central Asia into the fourteenth century, where their trail disappears. Numerous Gnostic sects and groups that were often simply referred to collectively as Manichaeans suffered a similar fate in Iraq. Only a small Baptist sect of the Mandaeans has survived in the marshy regions of southern Iraq.

As former provinces of the Roman-Byzantine empire, Syria, Lebanon, Palestine, and the Emirate of Transjordan – always referred to by Arabs as a single country, *al-Shām* – were Christian lands with Jewish and Samaritan minorities. They long retained this status even under the Muslim Arab rule, and to the present have maintained both the Monophysite Syrian ("Jacobite") and the Greek Orthodox ("Melkite") churches with their patriarchs, metropolitans, and bishops, and numerous churches and monasteries. The Church of the Holy Sepulcher in Jerusalem was always in Christian hands – except for a short interim between 1009 and 1020 under the Fāṭimid caliph al-Ḥākim. The Maronite church of Lebanon, named after the Syrian monk Maron (ca. 400), did not become independent until the eighth century under Islamic rule. A Uniate church, the Maronites are today the largest Christian group in Lebanon with their own patriarch.

In Egypt, the Arab-Islamic conquest ended the predominance of the Greek-Orthodox (Melkite) church, thereby alleviating the indigenous Monophysite Coptic (that is, Egyptian) church from extreme hardship. From then on the Coptic patriarchs of Alexandria led the Christians not only of Egypt, but also of Nubia, Sudan, and Ethiopia (Abyssinia). The new Arab metropolis of al-Fusṭāṭ (Old Cairo) became a bishop's seat. Egypt's population remained largely Christian, probably into the fourteenth or fifteenth century. Though the precise point in time cannot be determined, the scales began to tip as a result of a steady influx of Muslims – soldiers, officials, and Bedouins – and the attractiveness of Islam as the prevailing religion and the religion of the rulers. There was also occasional gentle pressure from above, especially on Coptic officials, who had dominated tax administration for centuries. Today the Coptic segment of the Egyptian population is estimated at about ten percent.

Christianity in the Maghreb – in contrast to Egypt and the Middle East – disappeared entirely, along with the Latin language. The Roman Catholic church offered less resistance, perhaps in part due to the gradual dwindling of Roman cities since late antiquity. The city of Thamugadis (Timgad) in present-day Algeria was already destroyed by Berbers in 485. The last bishop of Sitifis (Sétif) was mentioned in 525; the last one of Cuicul (Djemila), in 553. All of this happened long before the Islamic conquest, which perhaps merely continued, or even accelerated, a process that had been going on for centuries. In the late tenth century there were still forty-seven bishoprics in the Maghreb, fourteen of them in the southern part of present-day Tunisia. In 1095, however, Pope Leo IX lamented in a letter to the bishop of Carthage that "in all of Africa" only five bishoprics were still occupied. A short time later the Catholic church as an organization must have vanished entirely from the Maghreb, although St. Louis IX, King of France, did encounter a few Christians in Carthage on his crusade in 1270.

Al-Andalus, the Iberian peninsula, is a special case insofar as the Christian *Reconquista* started here immediately after the Islamic conquest. As a result, Islamic influence on the peninsula was gradually forced southward and in the thirteenth century limited to present-day Andalusia. The situation of the non-Muslim minority was no different here than in North Africa and the Middle East. Islam was the prevailing religion; Christians and Jews enjoyed the protected status of *dhimmīs*. There is no evidence that the atmosphere here was particularly tolerant or liberal in comparison to Asia Minor and the Middle East. The "Alhambra

Islam" frequently invoked by present-day authors is more utopian fantasy than historical reality. Nevertheless, minorities here were not treated more harshly than they were elsewhere. There were Jewish and Christian viziers and high-ranking officials here, as well as non-Muslim scholars.

The *Reconquista* had different consequences in the regions of Spain and Portugal that returned to Christian rule. In the eastern kingdom of Aragón the nobility was more tolerant with its new Muslim subjects, well aware of the economic repercussions their expulsion or extermination would bring. In contrast, the influence of the church and the orders of knighthood – the most important supporters of the conquest movement – prevailed in Castile, where policies of complete re-Christianization through forced baptism or expulsion were enacted. When Granada was conquered in 1492 by the "Catholic Kings" Ferdinand and Isabella, this policy was implemented throughout all of Spain under the influence of Cardinal Cisnero. There were revolts by Arabs and Berbers of Andalusia who were forced to convert but secretly remained faithful to Islam. This led to the decrees of 1609 to 1614 by which King Philipp III expelled all of the "Moriscos" from the peninsula. With them – almost 300,000 people – Islam and Arab influence disappeared entirely from the Iberian peninsula. Aside from Sicily, this was the most significant loss the Arab world was forced to accept.

The Mamluks

In the ninth century, an innovation developed in Baghdad under the 'Abbāsids that had enormous military, social, and political consequences for the Islamic world: the emergence of the military caste of the Mamluks.

The Arabic word *mamluk* is a passive participle of the verb "to own." A Mamluk therefore is someone owned by someone else, a slave. The word came into use for a new kind of soldier. This phenomena is specific to the Islamic world and exerted a decisive influence there far into the modern era. When Napoleon landed in Egypt in 1798, he was confronted by an army of Mamluks.

It was Caliph al-Mu'taṣim (833–842), a son of Hārūn al-Rashīd, who in 815 was the first to purchase Turkish slaves from central Asia when he was a prince. He gave them military training and used them as soldiers in his guard. In 832 he already had a core group of 4000 slave soldiers; after acceding to the throne he continued to buy slaves on a grand scale. They came from the nomadic Turkish tribes of central Asia, that is, from present-day Uzbekistan, Turkmenistan, and Kazakhstan, and were sold primarily at the market in Samarqand, where they were purchased by agents of the caliph. The young men, removed from their families and homeland, developed a personal loyalty to their new owner. Unlike the Arab soldiers, who had previously comprised the armies of Islam, they had no tribal ties. The new troops, however, proved to be

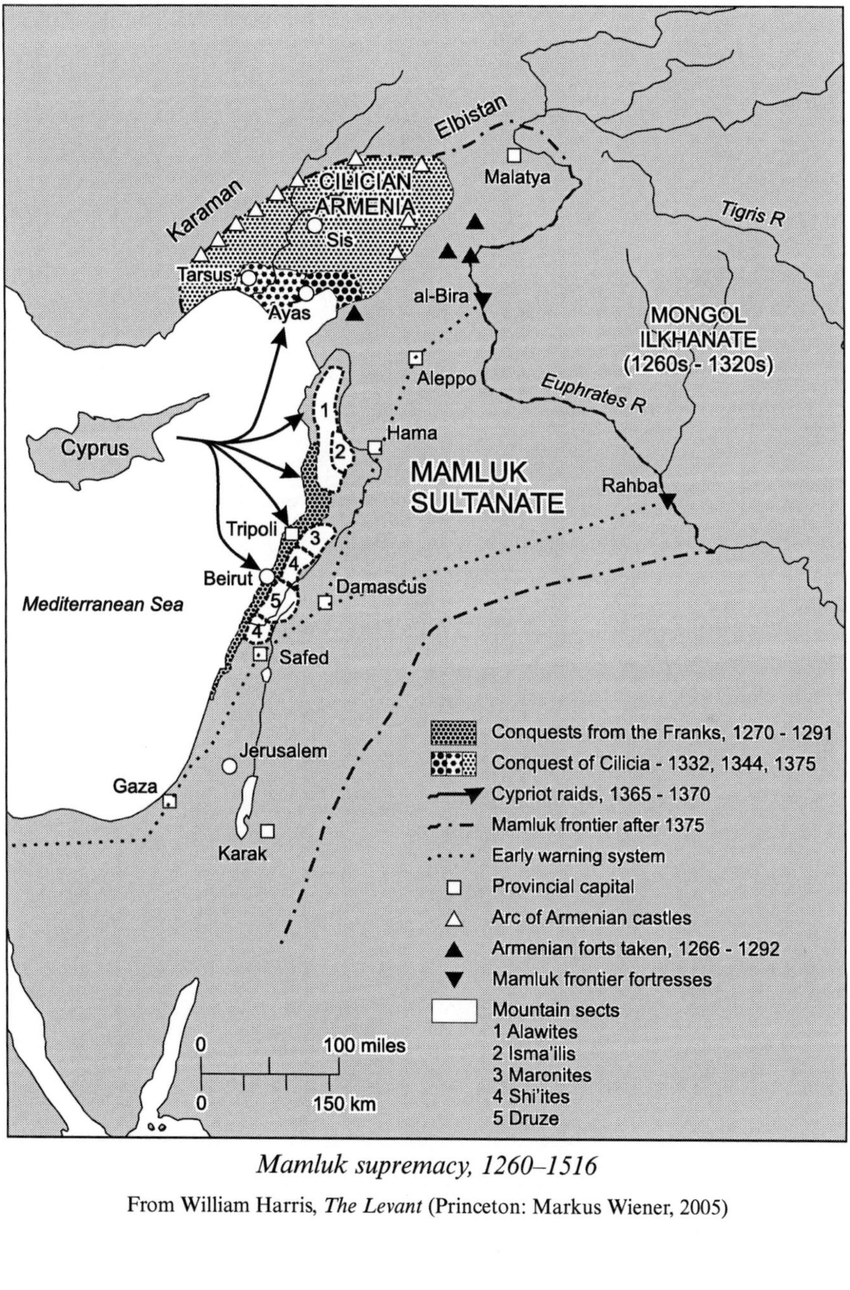

Mamluk supremacy, 1260–1516

From William Harris, *The Levant* (Princeton: Markus Wiener, 2005)

such an impediment in the metropolis of Baghdad and so onerous to citizens that in 836 the caliph established Sāmarrā, a new residence on the Tigris about seventy-five miles northwest of Baghdad, for himself and his new army. The next seven successors also resided there, expanding the Turkish army and the city, whose ruins extend today about thirty miles along the banks of the Tigris, making it one of the world's largest archaeological sites.

The new army soon developed a dynamic of its own. The soldiers imported as slaves were set free after a certain period of time and were then able to rise to the ranks of officers and generals or obtain positions in offices at court or become provincial governors. Al-Mu'taṣim ensured that soldiers were supplied with Turkish slaves as wives, so that the troops increased in number not only through purchases but through births as well. In Sāmarrā itself the army must have ultimately comprised about 20,000 men.

The disadvantages of this system, inherent to all praetorian guards, soon became apparent: The first generation of liberated slaves attained high offices and distinctions and began acting as kingmakers. They installed and deposed caliphs at will, even murdering them on occasion. When the 'Abbāsid caliphate threatened to sink into anarchy, Caliph al- Mu'tamid decided to move the court back to Baghdad in 892.

This new type of military continued to prevail, although it was never used exclusively. There were always units of free mercenaries as well from all over the world: Kurds, Iranian Daylamites from the southern shores of the Caspian Sea, Berbers or Arab Bedouins as light auxiliary troops. The Mamluk type of soldier, however, dominated not only the military, but also the political world – not only in Sāmarrā and Baghdad, but in Syria and Egypt too. Soon the kingmakers became kings themselves. In many countries, including Afghanistan and India, former slaves and their descendants assumed power and founded Mamluk sultanates. The most important of these was the Egyptian sultanate, which will be discussed below. In Spain and North Africa, the soldier slaves were not of Turkish, but of eastern European descent and were sweepingly referred to as "Slavs" (*ṣaqāliba,* sing. *ṣaqlabī).* They were brought primarily from across the Adriatic Sea.

The emergence of the Mamluks is significant primarily because for centuries they provided the Arab world with military and political elites who were of non-Arab origin and who, even if they adopted the Arabic language, retained an awareness of their foreign traditions. In the last millennium up to the present day, it has been more an exception than the rule that reigning houses in the Arab world were of Arab descent.

3

The Arab World from 900 to 1500 CE

al-Harīrī, *Maqāmāt*: Travelers arriving at a village (VII/13th century)

The year 909 CE marks an epochal year in the history of Islam. A caliphate was established in Tunisian Kairouan in that year that for the first time could challenge and rival the ʿAbbāsid caliphate in Baghdad on a long-term basis. The Fāṭimid dynasty, which claimed (albeit disputedly) to be direct descendants of Muḥammad's daughter Fāṭima and Caliph ʿAlī, was able with the support of the Berbers to assume control of present-day Algeria. In 910, ʿAbdallāh al-Mahdī, who had previously campaigned for himself in the underground, appeared openly in the city of Kairouan and assumed the title of caliph. His caliphate (909–934) was the first of an extremely successful dynasty that challenged not only the religious and political claims of the ʿAbbāsids in Baghdad to be Muḥammad's heirs; the Fāṭimid's Shʿite Ismaʿīlī sect of Islam also offered a religious alternative to the ruling Sunnīs. In 929, the Umayyad emir of Cordoba ʿAbd al-Raḥmān III (912–961) also assumed the title of caliph. This meant that three "successors" – two Sunnīs and one Shʿite – each claimed the exclusive heritage of the Prophet Muḥammad. The disintegration of the caliphate, which had in fact been long in the making, was now officially sealed.

Iraq

Mesopotamia, the land of the Tigris (*Dijla*) and the Euphrates (*al-Furāt*) rivers, consisted of two different landscapes for Arabs: the actual *al-'Irāq* – the name probably means "low lands" or "flat country" – in the southeast; and *al-Jazīra*, the "island," in the northwest between the middle reaches of the two rivers. The military camps of al-Baṣra and al-Kūfa, which had been established by Arabs, and the caliphate capital of Baghdad were located in Iraq. After the founding of Baghdad, Seleucia-Ctesiphon (*al-Madā'in* or "the cities" in Arabic), the ancient royal city of the Parthians and the Persians, diminished increasingly in significance. Babylon had already disappeared as a city even before the Islamic conquest. The metropolis of the north was Mosul (*al-Mawṣil*) on the Tigris, across from the ancient ruins of Nineveh.

As the seat of the 'Abbāsid caliph, the metropolis of Baghdad long remained the center of the Islamic world. After the turmoil in Sāmarrā and the emergence of the western caliphate, however, the political significance of the caliphs in Baghdad increasingly declined. While the 'Abbāsid caliph in Baghdad continued to rule without interruption until the Mongol invasion in 1258, only isolated representatives of this dynasty actually governed themselves and then only as a kind of Iraqi territorial prince. The Baghdad caliphate was repeatedly subject to the tutelage of military "patrons," who usurped political power and –

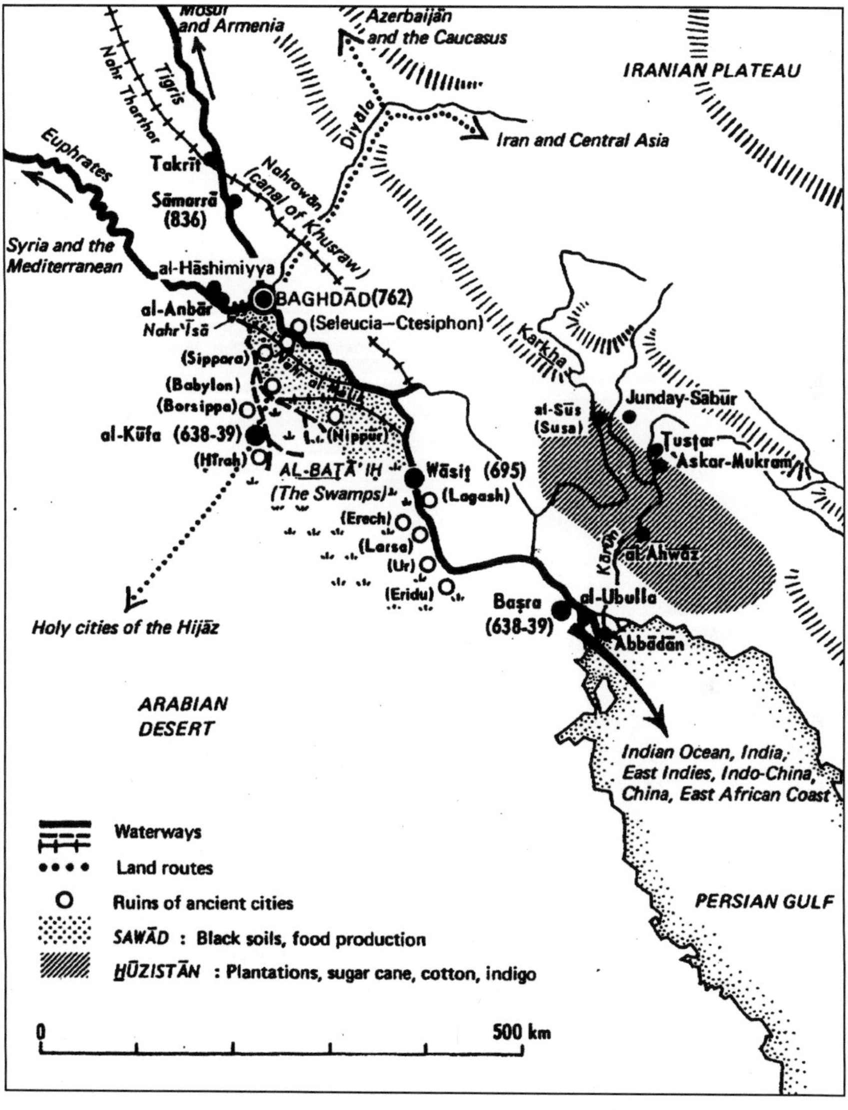

Mesopotamia

From *The Golden Age of Islam*

equipped with formal legitimation from the caliphs – exercised the real power for them. The focus of such rule lay primarily in Iran. Iraq was often little more than a western province of Iran.

The first patrons of this kind were the Būyids (932–1055), a widely branched Iranian condottiere family that established a series of dominions (Shiraz, Isfahan, Hamadan, Kerman) in western Iran and also seized power in Baghdad in 934. For 110 years, Būyids administered a protectorate over the caliphates, formally as commanders-in-chief (*amīr al-umarā'*) of the army, but in reality as sovereign rulers. They did not even eschew assuming the ancient Persian title of great king or emperor (*Shāhānshāh*, "king of kings"), which is completely antithetical to Islam. While the caliph had always been a Sunnī, the Būyids were Sh'ites and vigorously promoted members of this faith. A large portion of the Shi'a religious writings arose under their aegis. The burial places of their imams, which had been pilgrimage sites for Sh'ites for centuries, were expanded into magnificent shrines and received elaborate endowments: the grave of 'Alī in al-Najaf near Kūfa; the grave of the third imam (the Prophet's grandson al-Ḥusayn) near Karbalā'; the double grave of the seventh and ninth imams in al-Kādhimiya in the north of Baghdad as well as the graves of the tenth and eleventh imams in Sāmarrā; and the site at which the twelfth imam is supposed to have disappeared into "occultation" and from which he is expected to return.

The Būyids were overthrown by the Seljuqs, a Turkish dynasty that had forayed into Iran as the leaders of a wandering tribe of Turkish nomads from Central Asia. In 1038, their leader Toghril Beg had himself proclaimed sultan in eastern Iran, transforming the word *sulṭān*, which actually means "ruler," into a title. As the protector of Sunnī Islam, he compelled the Baghdad caliphs to officially recognize him and then appeared in Baghdad in 1055 with his followers to accept this recognition. The capital of the "Great Seljuq" Empire, however, was Isfahan in Iran, while Baghdad was left to the powerless caliphs.

With the Seljuq dynasty, Turks or Turkmen appeared for the first time in the Islamic world not as imported military slaves, but as larger tribal groups. A steady flow of Turkish tribes now moved westward through northern Iran. In 1071, the Turks succeeded where Arabs had continually failed: After defeating the Byzantine Emperor Romanus IV Diogenes at Manzikert (present-day Malazgirt north of Lake Van), the Seljuqs overran what had been Greco-Christian Asia Minor.

Although Baghdad lost its political significance under the Seljuqs, it remained a cultural center with enormous appeal and influence, particularly after the Seljuq vizier Niẓām al-Mulk (1065–1092), an Iranian, established a madrasa, a legal, theological institution of higher education based on Iranian precursors, and appointed the famous Sunnī theologian and mystic al-Ghazālī (1058–1111) as the institution's first professor. A large number of similar institutions quickly arose in Baghdad. The Mustanṣiriyya, founded by Caliph al-Mustanṣir in 1233, is today Baghdad's best-maintained monument from the pre-Mongol era. The work by the Sunnī jurist and preacher al-Khaṭīb al-Baghdādī (1002–1071) offers an excellent example of intellectual life in the caliphate capital during this period. His

Chronicle of Baghdad (*Tā'rīkh Baghdād*) – actually a lexicon of scholars – comprises fourteen volumes with entries on no less than 7,831 people active in the intellectual life of the city.

Even after the gradual disintegration of the Seljuq empire, Baghdad remained a strategic object in particular for eastern rulers, even if individual caliphs such as al-Nāṣir (1180–1125) were occasionally able to exercise their own rule on a regionally limited basis. The invasion of the Mongols, however, brought all of this to an end. In 1235, Hulagu Khan, grandson of Genghis Khan and brother of the Mongolian Great Khan Mongke, was ordered to subjugate the caliphate. When Caliph al-Musta'ṣim (1242–1258) refused to comply with official demands to support the Mongols with an army, the Mongols overran Iran from Oxus (Amu Darya) and attacked Iraq. In January 1258, the Mongols were outside Baghdad. The caliph, his vizier, and the Nestorian Catholicos – Hulagu's mother was Christian – attempted in vain to negotiate. On February 10, the Mongols forced their way into the city and began to burn, murder, and plunder. The caliph and many of his dignitaries and family members were strangled. Thus the caliphate, the succession of the Prophet Muḥammad, came to an end. Although the Catholicos and numerous mosques and madrasas were spared, the city itself did not recover from this blow until the nineteenth century. Iraq was incorporated into the Mongol Empire. Mongol rulers in Iran, the Il-Khan and their successors, quickly converted to Islam, but they resided in Iran and adopted Iranian Islamic culture. In Iraq, they were always regarded as foreign occupiers.

Syria/Palestine

Arabs believe that the territories of present-day Syria, Lebanon, Jordan, Israel, and Palestine constitute a unity they call *Bilād al-Shām*, the land to the left or land of the north, in contrast to Yemen, the land to the right or to the south. In political terms, however, this territory was divided into small cantons by its mountains and had never formed a unified whole, even under Islam. When regionalized political rule was established in the ninth century, the southern part – Palestine, Transjordan, and southern Syria including Damascus – was tied to the respective emirs ruling in Egypt, whereas northern Syria with its emerging metropolis of Aleppo (*Ḥalab* in Arabic) constituted an emirate onto itself under the dynasties of Bedouin origin, the Ḥamdānids (945–1004) and the Mirdasids (1023–1079). The Islamic emirate of Aleppo usually paid tribute to the Christian Emperor in Byzantium, although sometimes it was ruled as a joint Byzantine-Egyptian condominium, functioning as a buffer state between the Christian and the Islamic worlds. During this era, three Arab Bedouin groups exerted the decisive political pressure on the western horn of the Fertile Crescent. From the Transjordan, the Tayyi pressed across the Jordan River into Palestine in pursuit of grazing land, booty, and the recognition of their Sheiks as provincial governors; in the center, the Kalb pushed the Palmyrenes out of the oasis of Damascus; in the north, the Kilāb moved into Aleppo, which they ultimately also ruled as Mirdasid emirs.

This division of the region appeared to become firmly established when Turkish Seljuqs invaded Asia Minor from Iraq in 1071, expanding their rule into northern Syria, while the south remained under control of the Fāṭimids in Cairo. The first Crusade, however, altered this in a completely unforeseen manner. In June 1098, Crusaders conquered Seljuq Antioch (Antakya). On July 15, 1099, they took Fāṭimid-controlled Jerusalem and engaged in a terrible massacre of the Muslim population. Four western, Roman Catholic states were established: the county of Edessa with its epicenter east of the Euphrates; the Norman Principality of Antioch; the county of Tripoli under the Count of Toulouse at the foot of Mount Lebanon; and the Kingdom of Jerusalem – the most important of the four – with its alternating Lotharingian (later Lorraine) and French ruling houses.

The foreign rule of the "Franks" (*al-ifranj*), which lasted almost a century, met with no unified resistance from the Muslim side. Ibn al-Athīr (1160–1233), a historian from Mosul, complained bitterly about the disunity of the Muslims in his world chronicle *al-Kāmil fī al-ta'rīkh* (The Complete History). However, neither the Fāṭimid caliphs in Egypt nor the caliphs in Baghdad and their Seljuq protectors were in fact capable of preventing the transformation of Palestine, Lebanon, and large parts of Syria into Christian feudal domains.

Resistance was organized only when the emir of Mosul, Zengi (1127–1146), son of a Turkish Mamluk, was able to destroy the first of the four Crusader states by taking Edessa in 1144. His son and successor Nūr al-Dīn ("Light of Religion," 1146–1174) established his residence in Aleppo

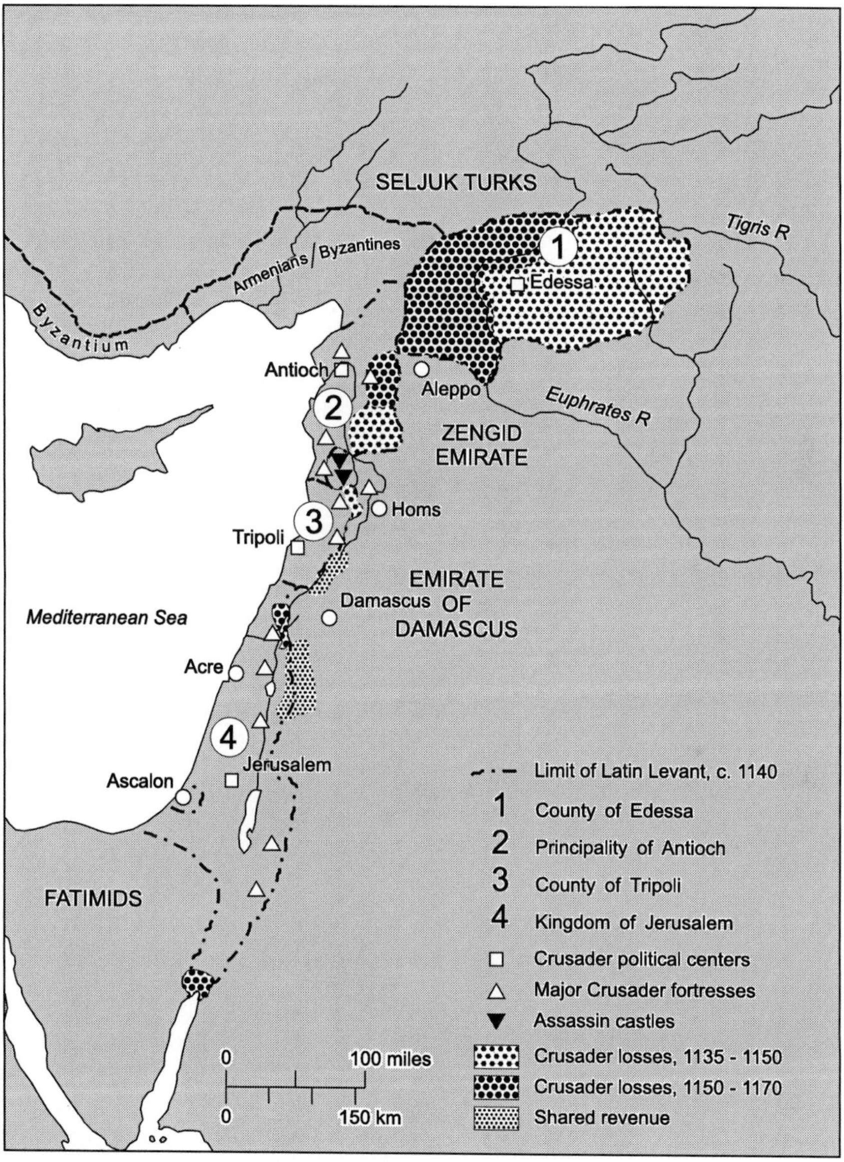

Crusader alignment, 1130–1170

From *The Levant*

and successfully continued the war against the Crusaders. In 1154, he was able to occupy Damascus, where a Seljuq emir ruled, without a fight. Then he attempted to bring Egypt under his military control, in rivalry with King Amalric I of Jerusalem. His success marked the end of Crusader rule. Yūsuf ibn Ayyūb, whose epithet was *Ṣalāḥ al-Dīn* ("Righteousness of the Faith," *Saladinus* in Latin), was a Kurdish military leader under Nūr ad-Dīn. He assumed power in Cairo in 1171 with the aid of the Syrian army, bringing down the Fāṭimid caliphate. After Nūr ad-Dīn's death in 1174, Saladin, as he was known in the West, proclaimed his independence from Aleppo and began to expand his power from Egypt to Transjordan, Syria, and northern Mesopotamia, and on to Mecca and Medina and Yemen. In a letter to Baghdad, Saladin justified his actions against the Muslim rulers there by pointing to the necessity of uniting Muslims in a just war or *jihād* against the infidels. The caliph provided him with a diploma of investiture for Egypt and Nubia, Arabia, Palestine/Syria, and the entire Maghreb, thereby legitimating Saladin's military conquests. After 1177, the new sultan adopted the title "Restorer of the Empire of the Commander of the Faithful" (that is, of the Baghdad caliph). The three remaining Crusader states were surrounded for the first time by a united Islamic empire, which would soon crush them. On July 4, 1187, Saladin's army defeated the Crusaders led by King Guy de Lusignan at Hattin (*Ḥiṭṭīn*) near the Sea of Galilee. Within a few months, Saladin had conquered almost all of Palestine. Jerusalem capitulated on October 2, 1187. After this, Syria/Palestine was united politically with Egypt.

Egypt

After the Arab-Islamic conquest in 641–42, Egypt became a province of the caliphate. Its emirs resided in the Arab military camp of al-Fusṭāṭ (or Fusṭāṭ Miṣr) in the south of what later became Cairo. The land was ruled by hereditary dynasties for two brief periods of time. The Turk Aḥmad ibn Ṭūlūn (868–884) from Sāmarrā was the first governor of the Tulunid dynasty, which ruled until 905. The Ibn Tulun mosque, which he erected next to his palace complex, still exists today. The Ikhshīdids ruled Egypt from 935 to 969. Their first governor, Muḥammad al-Ikhshīd, had also been a Turkish general.

However, Egypt did not become the center of a truly independent empire until 969, when after a series of failed harvests, epidemics, and other catastrophes the notables of al-Fusṭāṭ decided to transfer rule to the Sh'ite Fāṭimid caliph of North Africa, the fourth Fāṭimid ruler al-Mu'izz (955–975), who sent an army of Berbers and "Slavs" led by the freedman Jawhar. The army marched into Egypt in 969 and immediately began building a new capital city north of al-Fustāt, which the caliph entered from Tunisia in June 973. The new palace city was named "The Victorious of Mu'izz" (*al-Qāhira al-Mu'izziyya*). Under the rule of the Egyptian Fāṭimids (969–1171), Cairo (*Qāhira*), with its new Friday mosque the Al-Azhar (The Brilliant), became one of the largest metropolises of the Arab world, soon to rival Baghdad in size and importance. The fall of the

'Abbāsid caliphs in Baghdad remained the declared goal of the Sh'ite counter-caliphs in Cairo. Egypt's Muslim population – which was still a minority in comparison to Coptic Christians – remained Sunnī even under the Sh'ite dynasty.

Control over the holy sites of Mecca and Medina, with the attendant responsibility for protecting the annual pilgrimage (*hajj*), fell to the Egyptian Fāṭimids almost automatically. In contrast, they were forced to fight a hard battle for control of Palestine/Syria and even then were able to assert control only temporarily, particularly in Aleppo. Thanks to a rebellious Turkish general, Friday prayers for the caliph in Cairo were held in Baghdad for an entire year, 1059, before the Seljuqs were able to re-occupy the city. The Sh'ites were never able to restore this kind of unity to the caliphate. In the west, Cairo ruled at least nominally over what is today Libya and Tunisia and large parts of Algeria (where the Zīrid Berbers ruled the Maghreb for

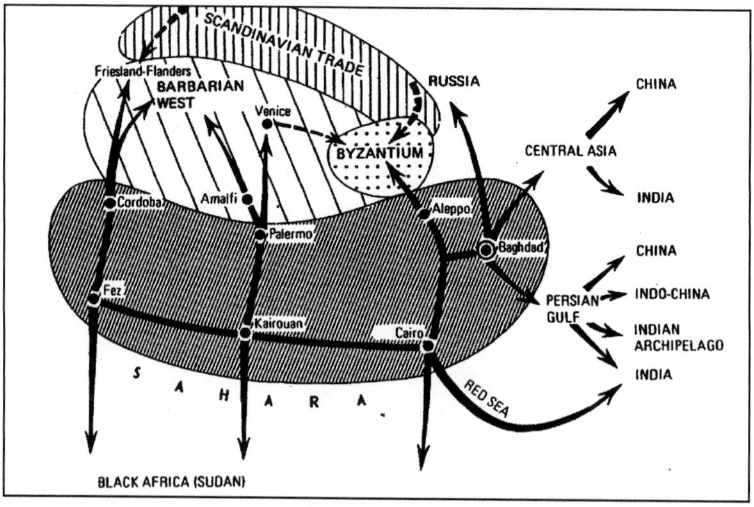

Trading connections of the muslim world

From *The Golden Age of Islam*

Cairo as a kind of viceroy), as well as over Sicily, whose emirs regularly had themselves reaffirmed in Cairo. Due to its control of the Red Sea and Yemen, Egypt became the hub of world trade at the time between the Indian Ocean and the Mediterranean. Immense wealth flowed into the country from this, as well as from surplus agricultural production, high-quality textiles, and the export of alum, a mineral in great demand, also in Europe, for tanning leather and which was mined as a state monopoly. Under the Fāṭimids, Italian maritime trading cities became active in the Levant – first Amalfi and Pisa, and later Venice and Genoa. This trade reached its apex during the Crusades.

The loss of the Maghreb in 1044 when the Zīrids established their independence did not weigh all too heavily against these Fāṭimid successes. The dynasty, however, did experience a serious internal crisis during the era of the Crusades. It lost not only its Syrian-Palestinian provinces, but was also occupied a number of times by armies of the King of Jerusalem, becoming a protectorate of the Crusaders. However, the fall of the Fāṭimids and Saladin's re-establishment of Sunnī orthodoxy in 1171, along with his subsequent unification of Cairo, Damascus, and Aleppo proved to be prerequisites for a resumed, even greater expansion of Egyptian power.

Saladin's victory over the Crusaders at Hattin in 1187 brought almost all of Palestine, including Jerusalem and the Syrian coast, under Muslim control again. The Franks led by King Richard the Lionheart of England and King Philip II (Philip Augustus) of France did retake Acre in 1191, and Emperor Friedrich II was even able to negotiate a restitution of Jerusalem from the Egyptian Sultan in 1229 without a struggle, so that only the Temple Mount with the Dome of the Rock and the al-Aqṣā Mosque remained in the hands of the Muslims. This intermezzo, however, lasted only until 1240.

The Saladin dynasty, the Ayyūbids (named after Saladin's father, Ayyūb = Job), was a dynastic ruling alliance. All the princes of the original Kurdish family were given provinces and ruled in continually changing constellations from Yemen to northern Mesopotamia. Cairo and Damascus remained the centers of Ayyūbid rule.

Sultan al-Ṣāliḥ Ayyūb (1240–1249), a great nephew of Saladin, reinforced the Mamluk troops in Cairo through extensive purchases of Turkish war slaves, establishing the Baḥrī (River) Regiment, which was named after their barracks on Roda Island in the Nile. This elite troop took advantage of French King Louis IX's Crusade against Cairo in 1249 to remove the Ayyūbid dynasty. One of the Mamluk officers, the Turk Aybak proclaimed himself Sultan and established Mamluk rule over Egypt, Palestine/Syria, and the holy shrines, which lasted until 1517. The Turkish Mamluks enjoyed several spectacular successes, which legitimated their usurped rule and bolstered their reputation as champions of Sunnī Islam. On September 3, 1260, at the "Spring of Goliath" ('Ain Jālūt) near Nazareth, they defeated the Mongols, whose vanguard had already pushed through up to Gaza. In 1261, the important Mamluk Sultan Baybars (1260–1277) named an 'Abbāsid prince, who had fled from the Mongols, "caliph" in Cairo. However, like his successors prior to 1517, this caliph had no real power and had only to "install" the respective Mamluk sultan. Baybars, who sought to complete Saladin's work, was also able to conquer the castles of the Isma'īlī assassin sects along the Syrian border between the Crusaders and the Muslims. In almost annual campaigns, the already diminished territory of the Crusaders was continually reduced further. Baybars re-conquered Caesarea, Ashkelon, Jaffa, Haifa, and Antioch. Under Sultan Qalāwūn, the city of Tripoli in Lebanon fell in 1289. In May 1291, his son al-Ashraf Khalīl was able to take Acre, the final base of the Crusaders on the Levant coast.

The rule of the Malmuks in Cairo (1250–1571) was one of the most remarkable and successful examples of state building in the Arab world. The Malmuk military aristocracy was, as Jerusalem historian David Ayalon writes, a "one-generation aristocracy": Only Mamluks brought in from outside – initially of Turkish and beginning in the fourteenth century of Circassian descent – could ascend the military hierarchy and ultimately become sultan. Their children were forced, at least as a rule, to take up civil professions. Many of them became scholars, who produced the abundant religious and secular literature we have about the Mamluk era. Despite the non-Arab origins of this elite, Egypt remained an Arab country, and it was almost certainly during the Mamluk period that Muslims for the first time constituted a majority of the population. This era still today has an influence on the city of Cairo. While work on the citadel began under Saladin, the majority of the mosques, madrasas, and mausoleums in the city can be traced back to endowments by Mamluk sultans and officers. Even after the Ottomans conquered Egypt, the Mamluk military aristocracy continued to lead the country.

The Maghreb and al-Andalus

No independent state developed in premodern times in what is today Libya. The two urbanized regions there in antiquity – the five cities of the Greek Pentapolis with its main city of Cyrene (Cyrenaica) and the three cities of the Roman Tripolis, Oea, Sabratha, and Leptis Magna – were separated by a great distance. While the former was administered primarily by Egypt under the name of al-Barqa, the latter lay within Kairouan's sphere of influence.

Under Arab rule, the former Roman provinces of Africa and Numidia were combined to form the region of Ifrīqiya, which encompassed not only Tripoli and present-day Tunisia but all of northeastern Algeria as well, including Constantine, Bône, and Bougie. The Arab city of al-Qayrawān (Kairouan), originally a fortified military camp, replaced the abandoned city of Carthage as the urban focus of the region, becoming a significant center for religion and the arts and sciences. Under the Aghlabid dynasty (800–909), which was nominally subject to Baghdad, Kairouan acquired a metropolitan character. The mosque of Emir Ziyādat Allāh I (817–838), which was completed in 836 and still exists today, became a model of architecture and architectural decoration for the entire region. The palaces and parks in Raqqāda (six miles south of Kairouan) have been uncovered by contemporary archeologists in extensive excavations.

The Aghlabids were driven out of Algeria by a Berber army in 909. A year later, the Fāṭimid ʻAbdallāh al-Mahdī proclaimed himself caliph in Kairouin. This Isma'īlī-Sh'ite dynasty brought the Maghreb ("the West" in Arabic) into open conflict with the Sunnī caliphate of the ʻAbbāsids in Baghdad. A new palace city, al-Mahdiyya, was built on the coast of a rocky peninsula, and another palace, al-Manṣūriyya (directly south of Kairouin), was erected later. After the peaceful assumption of power in Egypt in 969, the fourth Fāṭimid caliph al-Mu'izz settled in the newly founded city of Cairo in 973, leaving the Maghreb to his viceroy, the Zīrid Berber prince from Algeria, who moved into the abandoned Fāṭimid palaces.

When the Zīrids renounced their allegiance to Cairo in 1044 and returned to Sunnī Islam, recognizing the distant Baghdad caliph, it triggered an emigration westward by Arabic Bedouin tribes between 1050 and 1052 (see page 63), marking the beginning of the Arabization of southern Tunisia and the central Algerian steppe.

In Arabic, Morocco is called *al-Maghrib al-Aqṣā*, "the farthest west." Six successive Muslim dynasties have ruled Morocco up to the present. These dynasties have consistently drawn their power from indigenous Berber tribes, even if they themselves have for the most part been Arabs from the Middle East and Asia Minor. The model for this form of rule, which is typical for Morocco, was established by a political refugee, Idrīs, who was a direct descendant of Muḥammad's grandson al-Hasan. Idrīs established his rule around the old Roman city of Volubilis in 789, supported by the Awrāba, a Berber tribe. Idrīs's mausoleum in nearby Moulay Idriss remains a kind of national shrine for Moroccans even today. His son Idrīs II (793–828) expanded the city of Fez (*Fās*), which had been founded by his father, into a metropolitan center of Arab rule (see page 45). The Kairouan (al-Qarawiyyīn) Mosque in Fez became the country's religious and intellectual center.

Following the fragmentation of Idrīsid rule into a dozen local entities, the Tunisian Fāṭimids and the respective rulers in al-Andalus battled over control of Morocco. The country was then unified by Ibn Yāsīn, a pious man who had founded a monastery-like Islamic fortress or ribāt in southern Morocco. Warriors of the Sanhāja, a Berber people from the western Sahara whose men wore blue veils, gathered around Ibn Yāsīn and formed the militia of the "Ribat people" (*murābiṭūn*, in the Spanish derivative *Almorávides*), which was quickly able to conquer all of Morocco and the coast up into the area around Algiers. In 1062, their secular prince Yūsuf ibn Tāshfīn (1061–1106) founded Marrakech (Marrākush, in Spanish *Marruecos*, from which the current name Morocco is derived) as his capital, which, in contrast to Arab-influenced Fez, was a city of Berber-African character.

Yūsuf ibn Tāshfīn crossed the Strait of Gibraltar with an Almoravid army in 1086 to intervene in al-Andalus. The caliphate of Cordoba had ceased to exist in 1031, and the Islamic sphere of power there had splintered into more than a dozen regional "party kingdoms" (in Arabic, *mulūk aṭ-ṭawā'if*; in Spanish, *Reyes de Taifas*) in Malaga and Sevilla, Cordoba, Valencia, Toledo, and Zaragoza, and others. This period of numerous small courts was very rich in cultural terms. Poetry, science, and the arts blossomed. The al-Ja'fariyya Palace (in Spanish, *Aljafería*) near Zaragoza testifies even today to the magnificence of the *ṭā'ifa* princes. They were unable, however, to resist to the rising Christian *Reconquista*. The intervention of the Almoravids unified the dwindled al-Andalus once more under the Berber dynasty of Morocco. The advance of King Alfonso VI from Leŏn and Castile in 1085, however, led to the definitive loss of Toledo.

The Almoravids were strict Sunnīs. The reform movement of Ibn Tūmart (Berber for Ibn 'Umar), the Berber holy man from the High Atlas, opposed the Almoravids' dogmatic and legally ossified understanding of Islam and probably their customs as well, which were unfamiliar to Arabs, such as men rather than women wearing veils. Ibn Tūmart was able to win over the Masmūda farmers from the high mountains, who called themselves "The Monotheists" (*al-muwaḥḥidūn*; in the Spanish derivative *Almohades*), and came down from the High Atlas to topple Almoravid rule. When Ibn Tūmart – who was revered as the Mahdī ("The Rightly Guided One") sent from God – died in 1130, one of his students, 'Abd al-Mu'min (1130–1163), assumed leadership of the religious movement (regarded as heterodox by Sunnīs) and called himself caliph, successor, to the Mahdī Ibn Tūmart. This was the first time a non-Arab ruler assumed this sacred title, which until this time had been reserved for members of the Quraysh tribe from Mecca. After 1145, the Almohads subjugated all of al-Andalus that remained Muslim and defeated King Alfonso VIII of Castile at Alarcos (west of today's Cuidad Real) on July 18, 1196. It was the last important Muslim military victory against the Christian Spaniards. The entire Maghreb up to Tunis and Tripoli also came under Almohad rule; in particular the Bedouin Hilāl tribe was subject to this centralized rule.

The Almohad court was influenced by the culture of Cordoba. Especially the architecture of the epoch testifies to the predominant influence that the so-called "Moorish" art of Andalusia had on Morocco and Algeria. The great mosques of the Almohads, the Mosque of Tinmal in memory of Mahdī Ibn Tūmart in the High Atlas (1153), the Great Mosque of Tlemcen in Algeria (1136), the Kutubiyya (Booksellers') Mosque in Marrakech (around 1150–1196), the enormous mosque of Rabat including its unfinished minaret, the Ḥassān Tower (around 1190), the Great Mosque of Sevilla with its minaret, which today serves as a bell tower for the cathedral (1195; in Spanish, *la Giralda*, "the weathervane"), and the Torre de Oro (Tower of Gold) (1220) on the Guadalquivir River in Sevilla were all products of the Almohad epoch.

The court of the second Almohad caliph Abū Ya'qūb Yūsuf (1163–1184) became a center of scholarship and literature. He sponsored the astronomer, physician, and writer Ibn Ṭufayl (ca. 1100–1185) from Cadix, whose *Hayy ibn Yaqẓān* (Alive, Son of Awake) was the most important philosophical romance of Arabic literature: the story of a young man who grows up alone on a deserted island and who must develop his insights and capacities solely through his own intellect and reason. Translated into Hebrew as well as Latin (under the author's name Abubacer), the novel continued to be influential into the modern era in Europe. Ibn Ṭufayl drew young intellectuals from al-Andalus into his circle, including the jurist and Aristotelian philosopher Ibn Rushd (Averroës), who was born in Cordoba in 1126 and became a protēgē of Caliph Abū Ya'qūb Yūsuf. Ibn Rushd served the Caliph as a judge in Sevilla, Cordoba, and Marrakech (1183), where he then succeeded Ibn Ṭufayl as court physician. Under Caliph Abū Yūsuf Ya'qūb (1184–1199), Ibn Rushd fell out of favor in 1195, and all of his philosophical writings were burned. However, after being banished for a brief period of time, he was rehabilitated and allowed to return to Marrakech, where he died in 1198. Ibn al-'Arabī (1165–1240), the most important Arab mystic, also struggled with the intolerance of Almohad religious scholars. Born in Murcia, Ibn al-'Arabī left the Almohad Empire in 1204, finding refuge in Damascus after an extended journey.

The Almohads abandoned their heterodox religious doctrine voluntarily. In 1230, Caliph Idrīs al-Ma'mūn personally renounced the Almohad doctrine on the pulpit (minbar) of Marrakech cursed the Mahdī Ibn Tūmart, and proclaimed the return to Sunnī Islam. Even before the Almohads were defeated at Las Navas de Tolosa by a coalition of Christian kings from northern Spain, their decline was imminent. The cities of southern Spain now fell to the Christians in rapid succession, including Cordoba in 1236 and Sevilla in 1248.

Up to the end of the fifteenth century, three Muslim states determined the fate of the Maghreb and Andalusia. From Tunis, the dynasty of the Ḥafṣids – founded by the Almohad governor Abū Ḥafṣ, a student of the Mahdī Ibn Tūmart – ruled all of Ifrīqiya, that is, Tunis and eastern Algeria, between 1228 and 1574. The Banū Merīn (Merinids), a nomadic Zenāta Berber clan, came to power in Morocco and western Algeria. In 1216, they advanced from the

Sahara to Morocco, occupying Marrakech in 1269. Like their predecessors, Merinid rulers were the heirs of Moorish culture and the art of Andalusia. They also adopted the eastern institution of the madrasa, the legal, theological institution of higher education. The magnificence of Moorish architectural decoration, which had arisen in Cordoba, reappeared in the madrasas of the Merinid in Fez, Marrakech, and Meknes. The Merinids, however, no longer intervened in al-Andalus. Only the Nasrid dynasty in Granada (1230–1492), which attempted to maneuver between Moroccan rulers and Christian powers, remained Islamic. In 1492, the palace of Nasrid, the Alhambra (*al-Ḥamrā* = "the Red"), fell into the hands of the "Catholic Kings" Isabella of Castile and Ferdinand V of Aragon. It is no coincidence that the fall of Granada was contemporaneous with Columbus's mission and the discovery of the new world and thus with one of the dates marking the dawn of the modern era.

The historian Ibn Khaldūn (1332–1406) developed a theory about the rise and fall of Muslim empires based on the vicissitudes of Moroccan-Andalusian dynasties. Ibn Khaldūn was the scion of an old Arab family, which was originally from Ḥaḍramawt but had already settled in Sevilla in the eighth century, and later in Ceuta and Tunis, where Ibn Khaldūn was then born. The scholar led a checkered life, traveling to numerous minor courts in North Africa and then to Granada, before he ended up in Cairo, where he served in a number of positions as a judge, although he was also jailed repeatedly during this time. He began his historical work on the Berber with an extensive "prolegomena" (*Muqaddima*) investigating the laws of historical events.

According to the work, clan solidarity (*'aṣabiyya*) of tribal associations makes up the powerful driving force for the development and expansion of political power, and the inevitable weakening of such solidarity in urban settings ultimately leads to dynastic decline. Ibn Khaldūn is often considered the "first sociologist," and in fact his highly original work, which comprises three volumes in modern book form, is unparalleled in medieval literature.

4

The Arab World from 1500 to 1800 CE

Waterwheels at Hamah, Syria

From Charles Issawi, *The Middle East Economy: Decline and Recovery* (Princeton: Markus Wiener, 1995)

There is a widespread perception that in the early modern era and even in the late Middle Ages the Arab world – and the Islamic world as a whole – experienced a developmental rupture that is best described by terms such as "stagnation" or "decline." Muslims, according to this argument, failed to undergo particular developments that were fundamental for the history of Europe – the Reformation, the French Revolution, and the industrial revolution – and for this reason have remained "backward." This failure supposedly left Muslims both defenseless against European colonial intervention and unprepared for modernity (to which they are said to react with uncertainty and violence even today). A variety of different factors are mentioned as possible or ostensible causes for this "decline and stagnation," including the ossification of religious doctrines in Sunnī Islam during the late Middle Ages, the European discovery of the Americas and of sea routes to India with the accompanying shift in the world trade routes, and the lack of communal self-administration and self-reliance in Middle Eastern cities.

In a series of recent studies, historians have demonstrated that at least the thesis of general economic decline needs to be modified. In the sixteenth century, the Ottoman Empire possessed an expanding and tautly organized central state, which had abolished numerous borders and thus established an economic region and trade routes that it was quite capable of securing. Coffee trade across the Red Sea, which resulted in an economic boom especially for Egypt, compensated for the shift of the spice trade to routes around the Cape of Good Hope, which were controlled by Europeans. Silk production in the Levant also remained competitive for quite some time.

Nevertheless, it is indisputable that the age of discovery ushered in an epoch of unparalleled European global dominance. Almost the entire Islamic world gradually came under the political, military, or economic control of European nations. This fate, however, was not limited to the Islamic world. It also occurred in the Indian subcontinent, Southeast and East Asia, as well as in North and South America. It is therefore hardly possible to hold Islam responsible for this development. What instead requires explanation is the precise, unprecedented dynamic that allowed Europeans to subjugate the rest of the world. There is as yet no convincing and generally accepted account of this.

The Crusades can be regarded as a prelude to this development. They represent the first attempt by western Europe to resolve internal demographic, social, and economic problems through measures taken beyond its own borders. It is certainly no coincidence that ascendant trade municipalities such as Pisa, Venice, and Genoa, with their dynamic bourgeois merchant elite, were both the driving force and the benefactors of the "armed pilgrimages" to the Holy Land. The age of discovery also marked the beginning of the expansion of European interventions in North Africa and Asia. The Portuguese occupied Ceuta as early as 1415 and Tangiers in 1471. After taking Granada in 1492, Spain also sought to control the North African coast across the Strait of Gibraltar. However, the aspiring Ottoman Empire proved to be a worthy opponent for the Spanish monarchy.

The Fertile Crescent under Ottoman Rule

By the beginning of the fourteenth century, the small Turkish principality of the Ottoman (*'Uthmān*) clan in northwestern Asia Minor had rapidly developed into an important territorial state. In 1357, the Ottomans were able to establish a foothold on the Balkan Peninsula, crowning their conquests with the capture of Byzantine Constantinople in 1453. While all of this took place outside of the Arab world, Arabs were directly confronted with the new empire in the early sixteenth century. Sultan Selim I brought down the Mamluk dynasty in Syria and Egypt. After the victory over the Mamluks at Marj Dābiq north of Aleppo in August 1516, the sultan occupied all of Syria and Palestine and then, in 1517, Egypt too. The Sharif of Mecca immediately sent him the key to the Ka'ba.

Under Selim's successor Suleyman I (the "Magnificent") (1520–1566), Iraq was also incorporated into the Ottoman Empire. In 1534–35, Azerbaijan with its capital city of Tabriz and northern Iraq with Baghdad were occupied, and in 1546, the south with Basra as well. In 1552, the Ottoman army expanded into the eastern coast of Arabia, where the province of (Sanjak) al-Ḥasā (around Hofūf) was established. The Ottomans were able to assert their maritime predominance through two naval bases, one in Basra on the Persian Gulf and the other in Suez (*Suways*) on the Red Sea. Ottoman Turkish rule over the Arab countries of

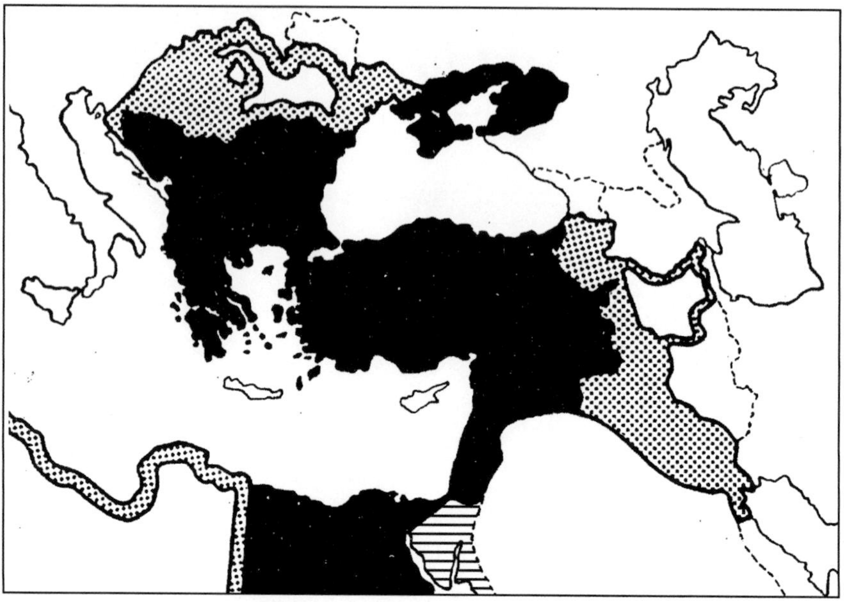

The Ottomon Empire

From *The Middle East Economy: Decline and Recovery*

the Fertile Crescent continued for the next four centuries until the empire finally collapsed during the First World War.

Turkish rule certainly had some positives aspects. The urban economy prospered, particularly in the trade center Aleppo. Damascus and above all Baghdad flourished again, after having endured numerous campaigns from Iran following the Mongol invasion. Centralized power in Istanbul, which remained unbroken in the sixteenth century, was maintained through strong governors (pashas), tax collectors, judges, and foreign garrison troops recruited in part from the Balkans. The unified legal system, codified under Sultan Sūleyman – whom the Turks called the "Legislator"

(*Qānūnī*) – and a tightly organized and highly efficient cadastral registration and tax assessment system were introduced everywhere. At the beginning of the seventeenth century, however, the reins began to loosen. The united elite, which as merchants and landowners had traditionally dominated economic and religious-intellectual life, began to (successfully) demand participation in political life. In Iraq, the governor Hasan Pasha (1704–1723) established his own de facto independence through his private army of Georgian and Circassian Mamluks, bequeathing his power to his son Ahmad Pasha (1723–1747). After this, outright Mamluk rule in Baghdad and Basra was established, which was tolerated and recognized by Istanbul and would continue until 1831. A similar situation developed in Mosul. In Syria, the local al-'Azm family played a comparable role from 1725 to 1807 as local governors recognized by the central government. Their palace in Damascus still testifies today to their wealth and magnificence. The pasha of Sidon, Ahmad al-Jazzār (1775–1804), whose fortress in Acre even Napoleon Bonaparte was unable to capture, ruled in a similarly independent manner.

The loosening of central power in the Ottoman Empire in favor of local and regional princes, however, did not automatically signify economic decline. While the empire itself was thrown into a serious crisis, the semi-autonomous provinces of the Arab world were able to thrive economically. As always, the Bedouins remained a disruptive factor, pushing repeatedly into settled territories in Syria/Transjordan as well as in western Iraq.

The Arabian Peninsula

In 1516-17, the Turkish Ottomans conquered Syria, Palestine, and Egypt, which meant that the Hijāz along with the cities of Mecca and Medina were also subject to the Sultan of Constantinople. In 1517, the Sharif of Mecca sent the key to the Ka'ba to Sultan Selim I and in return was confirmed in his office. From this point on, the Ottoman Sultan bore the title "The Custodian of the Two Holy Shrines" (*khādim al-ḥaramayn*), a title given to Egyptian Mamluk sultans prior to this (and used today by the king of Saudi Arabia). The sultan was now responsible for the support and care of the holy sites of Islam as well as for the organization and protection of the annual pilgrimage, the hajj, with pilgrim caravans from Damascus and Cairo.

Given its variety of starkly differing geographies, Yemen was not exactly predestined for political unity. Separate minor dynasties had been established in 'Aden, on the plains of Tihāma at the Red Sea, and in the metropolis of the highlands San'ā'. The most permanent force in Yemen was the Zaydī-Sh'ite imamate of northern Yemen with its center in Sa'da, which had been established in the ninth century and remained intact until 1962 – the longest-standing dynasty of the Islamic world. Its territory, however, did change over time. The Zaydīs repeatedly occupied San'ā', only to lose it and then reoccupy it again. In 1538, the Ottomans began to subjugate Yemen as well. They occupied San'ā' in 1546, compelling the imam to recognize the suzerainty of the sultan in 1552. Over time, however, the Ottomans were unable to sustain their rule, especially after European colonial powers appeared in the Indian Ocean and in the Red Sea – at first the Portuguese, then the Dutch and English. The Turks withdrew from Yemen in 1635.

Oman (*'Umān*) is separated from the rest of the Arabian Peninsula by deserts that long ensured its isolation. Since time immemorial, its coastal residents have been seafarers, who used the monsoons to reach the coasts of East Africa and India, making their living from maritime trade. In the sixteenth century, the Portuguese took control of the ports of Qalhāt and Masqaṭ (Muscat) in Oman as well as port of Hormuz (1514) on the Iranian side of the gulf. Oman remained part of the Portuguese colonial empire for a century and a half. In 1650, local Ya'rubīs were able to retake Masqaṭ. The succeeding Āl Bū Sa'īd dynasty (beginning in 1741) was able to expand its power to the island of Zanzibar off the African coast, giving rise to a remarkable double empire across the Indian Ocean.

In the eighteenth century, a form of political rule was established in the interior of the Arabian Peninsula that has continued, albeit with interruptions, to today: Wahhibism, the religious revival movement that led to the establishment of the Āl Sa'ūd monarchy (in Arabic, *Āl* = family; not to be confused with the article *al-*). The wandering preacher Muḥammad ibn 'Abd al-Wahhāb (1703–1792) sought to reestablish a pure and strict Islam true to its original form by opposing blasphemous "innovations" such as idolatry, the worship of graves, and the mysticism of the Dervish order. Only the Quran and sayings of the Prophet were supposed to guide Muslims. Support from the tribal leader

Muḥammad ibn Sa'ūd (died in 1765) ensured the dissemination of Wahhāb's teachings in the oases and among the tribes of central Arabia. As a result, Ibn Sa'ūd's son 'Abd al-'Azīz (1765–1803) was able to establish a powerful desert empire. The religious furor of the Wahhābīs was directed against the Sunnīs in Mecca and Medina, as well as against the Sh'ites in Iraqi Najaf and Karbalā'. The imam shrines of the Sh'ites were destroyed in 1802 by Wahhābīs armies, who also took Medina in 1804 and destroyed the al-Baqī' cemetery, where numerous companions of the Prophet and several Sh'ite imams had been buried. However, they did not dare to touch the Prophet Muḥammad's grave, although they did close it off to visitors. The Ottomans were unable to take direct action against these desert warriors. In a series of campaigns from 1811 to 1818, their Egyptian viceroy Muḥammad 'Alī destroyed this first Saudi kingdom, and in 1815, Ottoman rule over the holy shrines was restored.

Egypt

The Ottomans conquered Egypt in 1517, transforming it into a province of the Turkish Empire. New foreign elites appeared in Cairo, headed by the Turkish governor (*wālī*) who had the rank of a pasha and was accompanied by an army made up of the many nationalities within the Ottoman Empire. Especially the infantry of the Janissary corps (in Turkish, *Yeni Ḵeri*, "new troops") – comprised of Christian children from the Balkans forced into military service – were an increasingly important power factor. Egyptian Mamluks, however, were also employed in a new regiment.

The ties between the Egyptian province and central government in Constantinople were initially very close. However, the reins loosened over the course of time, as was also the case in Syria and Iraq. Access to power opened up again for local elites, as the foreign army was gradually "Egyptianized." In the seventeenth century, a Mamluk faction, the Faqāriyya, was able to rule Egypt for thirty years, limiting the power of the wali. In 1660, a rival faction, the Qāsimiyya, ousted the Faqāriyya. Something approaching a civil war ensued, in which the two sides crippled and almost annihilated each other, opening the way again for foreign intervention. The Janissary corps regiment was now able to control the country for an extended period of time and to defy the governor until the eighteenth century, when rivalry between Mamluk factions arose again. After 1760, Malmluk beys ruled the country, ultimately in a kind of duumvirate between rivals Ibrāhīm Bey and Murād Bey (whom Napoleon Bonaparte encountered upon landing in Alexandria in 1789).

A number of factors (such as the aforementioned coffee trade) testify to Egypt's prosperity during the time: Cairo's population doubled (from approximately 150,000 inhabitants in 1500 to about 300,000 in 1700); the city limits were extended; and a great variety of monumental buildings were erected during this era – mosques, schools, baths, caravanserais (Khān), and mausoleums. Of the many educational institutions in Egypt, the Al-Azhar Mosque in Cairo became the most distinguished in the late seventeenth century. Its elected leader, the *Shaykh al-Azhar*, came to be recognized as the foremost legal and religious authority, not only in Egypt, but throughout the Sunnī world.

The Maghreb

During the early modern era, the western Mediterranean served as the stage for antagonisms between the Christian maritime powers of Spain and Portugal on the one hand and the Ottoman Empire on the other. Through the use of its fleet, the Ottoman Empire attempted to gain control of the lands at the eastern and western ends of the Mediterranean by assuming the role of the protector of Muslims on the Iberian Peninsula (albeit without success) and in North Africa.

After taking Ceuta in 1415, the Portuguese continued their maritime expansion along the Atlantic coastline, occupying a series of bases on the Moroccan coast after 1458. The Spanish emerged as a naval power in the Mediterranean. The port cities of the North African coast became centers for a privateer war – understood as a *jihād* – against the Christian countries north of the Mediterranean. Booty and ransom were the economic motivations for these "Barbary pirates" of the Maghreb as well as for their Christian counterparts. After a raid by Moroccan corsairs on the Spanish cities of Alicante, Elche, and Malaga in 1505, the Spanish occupied all of the important ports of the Maghreb coast from 1505 to 1511: Marsā l-kabīr (Mers-el-Kēbir), Oran, Mostagānem, Tenes, Cherchell, an island off the coast of Algiers, Bougie, and Tripoli. In response, the Ottoman sultans encouraged and supported the corsairs by sending ships. Four brothers from the island of Lesbos (including the legendary Khayr al-Dīn, also known as Barbarossa) emerged as the leaders of this maritime enterprise against the Christians from 1504 to 1510. After 1516, Algiers (in Arabic, al-Jazā'ir, "the Islands") developed into a virtual corsair state under Khayr al-Dīn, tolerated by the Hafsid sultans of Tunis and supported by the Ottomans. Sultan Selim promoted the corsair to *beylerbey* (Turkish "bey of beys" for the Arabic *amīr al-umarā'*, "leader of leaders") with the rank of a pasha and provided him with troops and artillery. In 1534, he was able to occupy Tunis in the name of the Ottoman sultan. This success led to the intervention of Christian powers – Charles V sent his fleet to Algiers and Tunis in 1535 and Mahdia (al-Mahdiyya) was occupied from 1550 to 1554. In 1571, a Christian coalition of the Holy Roman Empire, the Papacy, and the Republic of Venice defeated the Ottoman fleet by Lepanto (Nafpaktos) near the entrance to the Gulf of Corinth, and in 1573, Don Juan de Austria took Tunis. Both were bitter setbacks for the sultan, but the Spanish were still unable to assume permanent control of the North African coast. In 1574, Sinan Pasha occupied Tunis from Tripoli. Spain decided to abandon the fight. In 1581, King Philip II agreed to an armistice with the Sublime Porte, ending the century-long power struggle and ceding North Africa to the Muslims.

The indirect Ottoman rule established in Tunis and Algiers led to curious polities. The Turkish army and fleet jointly ruled these two "regencies": Officers and captains sat together in the ruling councils (dīwān). In Tunis in 1591, a revolt of forty local officers with the Turkish title of *dey* ("uncle") removed the weak pasha from office. The deys placed one of their own in command, who then appointed the commander of the fleet (*qabtān* = "captain") and the bey, that is, the military officer responsible for collecting taxes from the local tribes of the interior. Throughout the entire seventeenth century, Tunisia was governed by deys, although the actual power gradually shifted to beys, who commanded their own troops. In 1705, there was a putsch by the agha (commander) of the *sipāhī,* the elite mounted force within the Ottoman cavalry divisions: Ḥusayn ibn 'Alī appointed himself bey and did away with the office of the dey. After 1710, the Husseinite dynasty ruled in Tunis as beys and struggled to transform the former corsair enclave into a modern state.

In Tripoli as well, local militia officers removed the pasha from power in 1603. A similar development also occurred in Algiers: Janissary officers (aghas), who dominated the divan, initially governed alongside the weak pasha. In 1659, the pasha's prerogatives were reduced to a merely honorary title with the Janissary officers rotating in a two-month cycle. After a military revolt in 1671, the deys elected by the militia headed the provincial government, which the Porte recognized as a sovereign state in 1711.

Morocco was the only country of the Maghreb that was able to avoid both Spanish and Ottoman rule, thanks to an Arab family from the south, from Sūs in the backcountry of Agadir. The Banū Sa'd were descendants of the Ma'qil Bedouins, who had immigrated to the Maghreb in the eleventh century. They formed an alliance with a marabout, a local spiritual leader, and in 1511 began to engage in a jihād against the Portuguese (who had occupied Agadir in 1505), subsequently expanding their power to the North over the High Atlas. In 1524, they captured Marrakech, where Sa'di graves in the magnificent mausoleum still testify to their power. They were able to take Agadir from the Portuguese in 1541, occupy Fez in 1549, and conquer corsair-ruled Tlemcen (*Tilimsān*) in western Algeria in 1550. An invasion by the Portuguese was thwarted in the Battle of the Three Kings in 1578, which took place at al-Qasr al-Kabīr (*Alcazarquivir* in Spanish). King Sebastian was defeated and killed in the fighting, as were the Moroccan pretender al-Mutawakkil and the Sa'di sultan 'Abd al-Malik.

The Sa'di dynasty disintegrated after attempting a massive expansion into the Niger region. The Alawites, the dynasty that continues to rule Morocco today, was able to achieve the renewed unification of the country. As their name implies, they are descendents of 'Alī and Fāṭima, the daughter of the Prophet Muḥammad, and thus Sharifs (the Arabic plural is *shurafā'*; in French, *chorfa*). Their progenitor was a descendant of the Prophet from the al-Hasan line who had immigrated to the Maghreb from Yanbu' on the Red Sea and settled in Rissani (Risānī) in the Tafilalt oasis at the eastern foot of the High Atlas in the early thirteenth century. The Alawite Sharifs ruled the Tafilalt oasis beginning in 1636, and proceeded to conquer the rest of the country from there. After taking Fez in 1666, Moulay (Mūlāy) al-Rashīd assumed the title of sultan. His brother Moulay (Mūlāy) Ismā'īl (1672–1727) succeeded him to the throne at age twenty-six and was the most significant ruler of the dynasty. He built Meknes (Miknās) into the new capital city and into a garrison for his powerful army, which consisted in part of sub-Saharan Africans, freed slaves, and Christian renegades. Moulay Ismā'īl drove first the Spanish out of al-Ma'mūra and al-'Arā'ish (Larache) and, after a five-year siege, the English out of Tangiers, which they had taken from the Spanish in 1622. The sultan was in fact able to subjugate almost all of Morocco, namely, that part of the country required to pay taxes to the central government (the "government lands," *bilād al-makhzan*), including the tribes on the High Atlas and the edge of the desert. In addition, the sultan was able to modernize the army and, like contemporary European countries, sought to institute a kind of mercantile economic policy that would stimulate and direct trade and the economy through directives from above. In doing this, his most important partners were the French King Louis XIV and his minister Jean Baptiste Colbert. The fact that after Moulay Ismā'īl's death his powerful state was again subject to riots and revolts demonstrates the actual lack of inner cohesion in the largely rural country, which was splintered into Berber and Arab tribal territories.

The "Moriscos," who had been driven out of Spain, contributed significantly to the economic prosperity of the Maghreb in the seventeenth century. In 1563, King Philipp II issued a ban prohibiting Moriscos (who had been forced to convert to Christianity but were in large part still secretly faithful to Islam) from possessing weapons without special authorization; and in 1566 he issued an edict banning Arab clothing and the veil as well as religious ablutions, ordering the surrender of all Arabic books and the exclusive use of the Castilian language within three years. Rioting ensued, particularly in Andalusia, between 1568 and 1571, which was quashed by force. Although many Muslims hoped the Ottoman fleet would intervene, it did not. Between 1609 and 1614, edicts were issued under Philipp III, authorizing the dispossession and expulsion of the Moriscos. While approximately 25,000 former Muslims remained in the country as Catholics, about 275,000 people left the Iberian Peninsula, seeking refuge in the various cities of the Maghreb. This influx brought life to North African cities, not only economically but also culturally. The Moriscos' contributions to art, architecture, and folklore are still recognizable in North Africa today.

5

The Nineteenth Century

The opening of the Suez Canal with Empress Eugénie of France, wife of Napoleon III.

From *The Middle East Economy: Decline and Recovery*

The Mashriq

During the nineteenth century almost the entire eastern (*al-Mashriq*) part of the Arab world – the Fertile Crescent, Egypt, and segments of the Arabian Peninsula – remained part of the Ottoman Empire, even though it was sporadically interspersed with various autonomous regions. The Arab countries were therefore subject to decisions made in Constantinople and increasingly to those in other European metropolises as well. They were greatly exacerbated by the crises of the Ottoman Empire, which had to accept significant territorial losses in the Balkans and north of the Black Sea. Just as consequential were the sultans' reform efforts starting in 1792 and the growing political, military, and economic influence of the major European powers.

A summary of all the developments of the Ottoman Empire would exceed the scope of this book; only the milestones of its development can be mentioned here: army reform based on the European model by Selim III (1789–1807) and the violent eradication of the Janissary corps (1826); Gūlhane's reform edict of 1839, the *Hatt-i Sherīf* ("noble edict"), declared in response to pressure from Europe, which for the first time made Muslims and non-Muslims equal before the law; the "reorganization" (*tanzīmāt*) of the legal and educational systems based on a new reform edict, the *Hatt-i Humayun* ("imperial edict") of 1856; the creation of a civil code, the *Mejelle* ("code," 1870–1876), which applied to the entire Ottoman Empire and continued to be effective after the collapse of the empire; and the introduction of a constitution in 1876 and the convening of the first Ottoman parliament in 1877, which, however, was suspended after only two short sessions in 1878 by the autocratic sultan ʿAbdul hamīd II (1876–1909).

Prior to the First World War, a consensus existed among the major powers of England, France, Austria, and Prussia/Germany not to contest the territories of the Ottoman Empire, which in particular was intended to prevent Russia from gaining control of Constantinople and the Balkans. Greek independence in 1829 was the only exception. The European powers even helped the Ottoman government, the Sublime Porte (*Bāb-i ālī*), in securing its rule over the Arab countries, preventing in particular the emergence of a major Egyptian kingdom. In return the Ottomans opened their empire to the trade interests of the major powers, which led the Porte to become increasingly dependent on the Europeans. This development culminated in the Anglo-Ottoman trade agreement of 1838, the empire's bankruptcy in 1875, and the establishment of an international debt administration (*Administration de la dette publique ottomane*) in Constantinople in 1881.

Iraq. Mesopotamia, which was largely rural, remained to a great extent a domain of Arab nomads, the Bedouins, into the nineteenth century. In the few urban centers, local dynasties were established, which were then tolerated by the Porte: in the north the Jalālī emirs in Mosul; in the south the Mamluks of Georgian descent in Baghdad, who also controlled the port city of Basra. Nevertheless, the Porte removed the local rulers in 1831 through a military intervention and reinstated the direct administration of Iraq. One of the most significant governors and modernizers was Midhat Pasha (1869–1872), Grand Vizier (1872), and Minister of Justice, and the father of the constitution of 1876, who later became governor of Damascus (1878–1880).

The cities along the Euphrates, al-Najaf and Kerbelā (Karbalā), had special status. The two holy Sh'ite shrines, the tombs of 'Alī and his son al-Ḥusayn, had attracted numerous Sh'ite clerics and scholars from Iran in the eighteenth century and developed into centers of Sh'ite jurisprudence and theology. Because the Sh'ites in the two cities remained largely to themselves, the Sunnī Ottomans didn't intervene, but when the Ottoman administration started forcing the nomadic Bedouins of southern Iraq to settle, the Sh'ite clerics found fertile missionizing ground among the tribes that had been only superficially Islamized. Within only a few decades, all of southern Iraq became Sh'ite, and the shrines found a loyal and generous clientele among the tribal sheikhs cum landed gentry. A tight symbiosis, often reinforced through marriage, developed between the clergy of the two shrines and the rural population of southern Iraq, which has continued to today.

Syria. The history of Greater Syria (*bilād al-Shām*) started in the nineteenth century with Napoleon's failed advance from Egypt, which was stopped by Ahmad Pasha al-Jazzār's defense of Acre. The Porte maintained its Syrian provinces and was even able to push back the local forces to the benefit of the central government. In Damascus the supremacy of the al-'Azm family ended in 1808. Although Greater Syria came under the control of the Egyptian pasha Muḥammad 'Alī (see pahe 126) in 1831, he was forced to abandon his conquests in 1840 due to pressure from England and Austria, which had come to the aid of the Ottoman Empire.

Lebanon assumed an exceptional position, having been a refuge for religious minorities since time immemorial. The Maronites controlled the north of the mountainous region; this Christian community was a Uniate church and had maintained close ties to western Christianity and France since the Crusades. Under their emir Bashīr II al-Shihābī (1788–1840), the Maronites established the foundations for their centuries-long dominance in the mountains of Lebanon, especially at the expense of the Druze settling in the southern parts of the mountains, a splinter group that had broken off from the Sh'ite Isma'īlīs. Maronite attempts to expand to the south had already resulted in heavy fighting between the two Arab groups several times in the nineteenth century (1841–45, 1860). In response to pressure from France, an autonomous province of Mount Lebanon was established in 1861, albeit without the port cities. With France's protection it continued to exist until the end of the Ottoman Empire. The Arab Christian population (Maronites, Greek-Catholic or Uniate, and Greek-Orthodox) outnumbered the Muslim minorities (Druzes, Sunnīs, and Sh'ites). After the First World War, Mount Lebanon became the nucleus of the Republic of Lebanon, which the Allies wanted to maintain as a Christian state and a European sphere of influence.

Arabia. The invasion of Iraqi Kerbelā in 1802 by the Wahhābīs under the leadership of the Sa'ūd family, as well as the conquests of Medina in 1804 and Mecca in 1806 (see page 109-110) directly affected the interests of the Ottoman Empire and introduced the sultan as the "Custodian of the Two Holy Shrines." Egypt's pasha, Muḥammad 'Alī, was ordered to challenge the Wahhābīs. After expanding his army he was able to retake Mecca and Medina in 1811–13, and in 1818 he even succeeded in capturing and leveling Dar'iyya in central Arabia, the stronghold of the Wahhābīs and the Sa'ūd family. Emir 'Abdallāh ibn Sa'ūd was deported to Constantinople and executed there. Egyptian-Ottoman control of central Arabia, however, could not be maintained in the long term and the Sa'ūd family was able to reestablish its control only a few years later, albeit on a local scale. The Ottomans used this opportunity once again to consolidate their rule in the Ḥijāz and along the coast of Red Sea. In 1872, Yemen too was returned to Ottoman control.

The Ottomans were forced to accept the fact that the British had established themselves throughout the Arabian Peninsula. In 1839 the East India Company took control of Aden, an important station along the route to India and a base at the entrance to the Red Sea, although its ultimate significance only became evident after the Suez Canal was built. The tribes of the hinterlands became tied to Britain through treaties. A similar development took place on the Arabian gulf coast starting in the 1820s. The conclusion of a permanent truce in 1853 transformed the "Pirate Coast" into the Trucial States, a British protectorate (since 1971, the United Arab Emirates). Of particular significance was the 1899 Anglo-Kuwaiti agreement between Britain and Sheikh Mubarak. The Porte considered Kuwait the end station of a Baghdad railway that had been in planning since

1888, which was to connect the capital, Constantinople, with the Persian Gulf. Because the railroad was being built by an Ottoman-German consortium, the British feared the German Empire could use this to gain influence at the gulf, so it strengthened its ties with the sheikh family of Āl Sabāḥ in 1899 through a treaty of protection that de facto released the city-state from the Ottoman Empire. This step would have repercussions in 1990–91 in the Kuwait conflict.

Egypt. During the first half of the nineteenth century, Egypt was certainly the most important Arab country. Although the significance of the landing of Napoleon's army in 1798 was greatly exaggerated with respect to the Islamic world in general, for Egypt itself it represented a major turning point. The French army, which was modern as in terms of both structure and weaponry, defeated the Mamluks at the pyramids. For the first time, the Egyptians were confronted with an efficient administration, modern jurisprudence, and modern scientific methods and instruments. Shock and admiration of this innovation are reflected in the diary and chronicle of the Cairo intellectual and scholar, al-Jabartī (1753–1825).

After the British and the Ottomans had forced the French to retreat in 1802, the Porte again appointed pashas as governors in Cairo. A violent coup in 1805 installed Muḥammad ʻAlī, an Arnaut (Albanian) from Macedonia, as pasha. His reign (1805–1848) is considered one of the most notable epochs in Egyptian history. After he had three hundred Mamluks massacred in the citadel of Cairo in 1811, he began building up a modern army and initiated a series of reforms that transformed Egypt for a time into a major power of the eastern Mediterranean and the Red Sea. He brought European technicians, consultants, and instructors to the country, especially from France, and sent students to Paris. Most importantly, Muḥammad ʻAlī revolutionized Egypt's agriculture. Cultivation methods were improved, irrigation was expanded, and cultivable land was increased. Production focusing on exports (wheat, rice, sugar cane) was promoted and, finally, starting in 1821 a cotton monoculture was created, which for a short time brought in rich yields, but also made the economy prone to crises. The state also tried to achieve a monopoly, not only in the area of agriculture, but also in manufacturing and the beginnings of industrial production and in trade.

Through this centrally planned and forcibly imposed economic policy, Muḥammad ʻAlī created the basis for a huge army, which grew to over 150,000 soldiers and served as a means of imperial expansion aimed at obtaining raw materials. After defeating the Wahhābīs in Arabia, the Egyptians conquered Sudan in 1820–23, which remained aligned with Egypt until the end of the century. From 1822 to 1827 the Egyptian fleet and army, in agreement with the Porte, intervened in the Greek war of independence. The pasha's goal was to control Cyprus, Crete, and the Peloponnese (Morea), but his fleet was annihilated in 1827 in the Bay of Navarino by the allied fleets of the British, French, and Russians. By invading Syria and Asia Minor in 1831 he started pursuing his own power politics at the expense of the Ottoman Empire. The Egyptians were able to take Greater Syria and Cilicia (with Adana and Tarsus) in 1831–1840. England and Austria, acting in their own self-interest, came to the assistance of the Porte, forcing the

Egyptians to abandon their conquests (except for Sudan). England wanted to prevent the emergence of a major Arabic power that might obstruct its trade interests and could threaten its ties to India.

Muḥammad ʻAlī's Egypt is often compared with Japan during the era of Emperor Meiji (1868–1912), who attempted a similar experiment in forceful modernization and emancipation from European influence, and succeeded. Egypt under Muḥammad ʻAlī was indeed the leading Arab country economically, technologically, and militarily. The fact that it failed here was certainly primarily due to European – especially British – intervention, although the structural weaknesses of the country, which were covered over by the forcibly imposed economic prosperity, certainly also played a significant role.

To some extent as compensation for the shattering of his plans to become a great power, Muḥammad ʻAlī was assured the succession of his sons and grandsons, who were confirmed as pashas by the Porte. His son Saʻīd ruled from 1854 to 1863, followed by his grandson Ismāʻīl, who reigned from 1863 to 1879 and received the title of khedive (Persian *chadīv* = viceroy) from the sultan in 1867. The Suez Canal was planned during the reign of Saʻīd and built from 1859 to 1869. It was a project that led within two decades to the ruin of the Egyptian state finances and the country's loss of independence. In contrast to Muḥammad ʻAlī, who had prevented any and all foreign intervention, his successors opened Egypt up to all European influences and especially to European capital, since they hoped Egypt would thus catch up with the major European powers and allowed to enter their ranks, as reformers of the Ottoman

Empire in Constantinople also hoped at the time. In fact, however, Egypt fell prey to foreign trade and money interests. An international pack of financiers, investors, and speculators exploited the opening of the country and sought their profits in a new El Dorado of the Middle East. Sa'īd Pasha's most egregious error was to let himself be talked into acquiring forty-four percent of the Suez Canal stocks, which threw him deeply into debt. In order to cover his short-term financial obligations he had to take out a long-term government bond on a London bank, for which he mortgaged the tax revenue of the provinces of the Nile delta. Because the debts could not be paid off, they accumulated astronomically under his successor Ismā'īl. On top of that came Ismā'īl's ambitious plans to modernize the country and his attempts to create an Egyptian imperium on the upper Nile and in equatorial Africa, in Eritrea and Abyssinia. More and more long-term government bonds had to be purchased, with growing concessions. The revenue earned by the recently built Egyptian railroad was mortgaged, as was the income of the private domains of the khedives. The astronomical level of the national debt ultimately led to the country's financial ruin in 1876 and the forced appointment of French and English financial controllers (dual control), who were responsible for monitoring all of Egypt's financial affairs. In 1876, the state debt administration came under foreign control with the establishment of the *Caisse de la dette publique*. The same thing happened five years later in Constantinople. A new, so-called "European" government was formed in Egypt in 1878, as an Englander ran the financial department and a Frenchman became Minister for Public Works.

Now the resistance of the khedives and local officers and notabilities was aroused, but the European powers forced the Ottoman sultan to depose Ismā'īl and to name his son Tawfīq (1879–92) as his successor. In early 1882 the opposition, led by Aḥmad 'Urābī and supported by Egypt's large landowners and businesspeople, succeeded in taking power for a short time in Cairo and temporarily forcing out the foreign Mamluk, Turco-Circassian elite. However, as early as September of that year British troops occupied the country.

The Maghreb

The fates of the three North African regencies that formally belonged to the Ottoman Empire (Tripoli, Tunis, and Algiers) took a similar course, though with considerable chronological delays. In the phase of dīwān rule, the council (*dīwān*) of officers of the Ottoman fleet and army governed the port city and its environs. This period was followed in all three by the establishment of a dynasty that developed from the dīwān and which over the course of the nineteenth century came under economic and military pressure from Europe and were ultimately forced to give way to direct colonial rule.

This development was first concluded in Algiers. There, the French took advantage of an incident to intervene in 1827. The dey of Algiers is reputed to have hit the French consul with a flyswatter. After a lengthy blockade of the port, French troops occupied Algiers in June-July 1830 and forced the dey, Husayn, to step down. The Bourbon king Charles X was still reigning when the coup occurred, but even the constitutional monarchy of Louis Philippe, the "Citizen King," and, after 1871, the Third Republic continued to control the country under pressure from the military. In the face of vehement resistance, Constantine was taken in 1837, but the Tuat oases in the southwestern corner could not be occupied until 1900.

The dynasty of the beys in Tunis solidified its rule by abolishing the Janissary corps at the beginning of the century, similar to Muḥammad ʻAlī in Egypt. The Mamluk officers of Circassian descent continued to comprise the military and political elite. Tax reform and even the brief experiment with a constitution (*dustūr*) and a parliament (1861–64) – albeit a powerless one – were supposed to modernize the country and relieve the pressure from Europe. But like the situation in Egypt, the policy of purchasing government bonds in Europe led to a growing national debt starting in 1863, and in 1869 a financial commission was appointed to look after the interests of the European creditor nations of France, Italy, and Britain, thereby undermining the state authority. The era of Khayr al-Dīn Pasha (1869–1879), an Abkhas from the Caucasus who sought to modernize the country in the style of the Ottoman tanzīmāt reforms, instead led to an even greater influx of foreign capital into the country. The situation rapidly worsened and, ultimately, the French occupied Tunisia in 1881 in order to forestall the colonial ambitions of a recently united Italy. Under their protectorate – the bey remained in office – the country now opened to European settlers, especially the French, but also Italians, who immediately started acquiring estates and engaging in agriculture and viticulture in grand style.

In Tripoli the dynasty of the Qaramanli pashas (starting in 1720) had already been eliminated by the Ottomans in 1825, who turned the semiautonomous regency back into a directly administered province. This move was an attempt to counter Egypt's independence efforts under Muḥammad ʻAlī and the French conquest of Algeria. As a result, European influence remained very weak in Tripoli. Not until the Italian conquest of Libya in 1911–12 did it become part of North Africa's colonial framework.

In Morocco, too, direct colonial rule was not established until the early twentieth century. The sultans of the 'Alawid dynasty in fact had control only over the Atlantic coastal plain with the four royal cities of Fez, Meknes, Rabat, and Marrakech, and over a territory that often fluctuated in size and in which the central government was able to levy taxes with the help of loyal tribes. This area was called the *makhzan* (literally "warehouse, magazine") and its size varied according to the momentary political constellation. Powerful regional princes (*qā'id,* "leaders") and monastery-like centers (*zāwiya,* "corner, hermitage") run by religious orders (*tarīqa,* plural *turuq*) exercised power in certain regions that proved difficult if not impossible for a centralized authority to control. France and Spain agreed in 1904 to divide up the country into spheres of interest. The German Empire had similar ambitions, but these were quashed at the Algeciras Conference in 1906. When in March 1912 the French set up their protectorate covering most of the country, Morocco was divided. The north became a Spanish protectorate and the port city of Tangier obtained international status.

Strategies against European Intervention: Europeanization, Islamic Renewal, Nationalism

Local elites in the Middle East and North Africa clearly recognized the pressures exerted by the European powers starting in the nineteenth century and correctly assessed the ensuing dangers. There was no scarcity of attempts to resist the growing foreign control. Reforms in the Ottoman Empire, in the largely autonomous Egypt, and in Tunisia sought to institute a forced modernization, or even Europeanization. They hoped in this way to catch up to Europe, which was becoming increasingly powerful – economically, politically, and militarily – and to be accepted into the community of nations as equal partners. This failed to occur due to the Europeans' own interests, which put greater value on opening markets for their own industries than on allowing potential competition to emerge.

The policies pursued by both the Ottoman and the Egyptian governments to open up to Europe nevertheless had positive effects as well. In the Fertile Crescent and in Egypt, the amount of productive agricultural land increased considerably; in Iraq, the increase was even tenfold, as a result of settling the Bedouins. The construction of the first Aswān High Dam on the Nile in 1902 made agriculture independent of the fluctuating peaks in the annual flooding of the Nile. Telegraph networks and railroad lines made vast areas accessible – just a few examples should suffice here: the Baghdad railroad line (1888–1940) and the Ḥijāz line (1900–1908), which connected Damascus and Medina and was intended to continue on to Yemen via Mecca. Steamship navigation connected waterways, which was particularly significant on the Tigris and the Euphrates; the construction of the Suez Canal eliminated the need for maritime trade routes around the Cape of Good Hope. Turkish and Arabic print media emerged. The flip side was that opening up to foreign capital, which largely financed these improvements in infrastructure, came at the expense of local trade, crafts, and agriculture.

European investors and entrepreneurs were not the only beneficiaries of the increased agricultural land area and intensified cultivation; local elites profited as well. A new class of local wealthy bourgeoisie and large landowners developed in the nineteenth century in the agrarian countries of the Middle East. Prior to the upheavals in the 1950s the notabilities came from these social classes and held political sway. In addition to these groups, who remained attached to the cultural and religious customs of their native roots, an elite developed in all of these countries which was oriented toward Europe and distanced themselves rigorously from the popular masses and their traditional ways of life, especially in the rural areas. This division of society, which of course also includes intermediate stages, has remained characteristic of Middle Eastern societies to today.

Europeanization was opposed especially by those segments of the population that viewed themselves as victims of the process, including the urban middle classes, the farmers, and the Bedouins. Countering the powerful foreign influences with something of their own meant returning to established traditions, especially Islam. Since the foreigners were perceived primarily as Christians, their own self-definition as Muslims was an obvious connecting link. In numerous places, charismatic religious leaders organized resistance, which was open to everyone who saw their status threatened by the rapid social changes.

Armed resistance first formed in places where the colonial power was immediately evident in the form of military troops. Thus the French in western Algeria encountered the resistance from the irregular militias around ‘Abd al-Qādir, son of a sheikh of the mystical Qādiriyya order, who in 1832 called himself the "Sultan of the Arabs." The French had recognized him in a number of agreements and treaties as the leader of a partly independent west Algerian state, but when he started to constantly expand his sphere of power and declared *jihād* against all non-believers, the French opposed him with military strength from 1840 to 1847, ultimately forcing his surrender. He spent the rest of his life writing mystical works in exile in Damascus (1883).

The revolt of the Mahdī in Sudan was similarly rooted in the traditions of the mystical orders (*turuq*). The forty-year-old sheikh Muḥammad Aḥmad claimed in 1881 to be "The Rightly Guided One" (*al-mahdī*), the savior and redeemer of Islam sent by God and anticipated by all Muslims. He vowed to expel the non-believers, referring to the British, whose General Charles Gordon had led a merciless regiment from the Sudanese capital of Khartūm (Khartoum), expanding Egypt's sphere of power – in reality Britain's – as far as equatorial Africa from 1874 to 1879 in the name of the khedive. The Anglo-Egyptian Convention of 1877 played a significant role in the rise of the Mahdī. The convention abolished slavery in Sudan, which was a powerful blow to the slave traders and holders there. Corresponding to his title, the Mahdī appeared as the renewer of Islam. His supporters called themselves *anṣār,* or helpers, based on the model of the Prophet Muḥammad's supporters in Medina. In the province of Kordofan, an Islamic state headed by the Mahdī emerged. Gordon, who in 1884 was redispatched by London, was killed in January 1885 when the Mahdī's soldiers stormed Khartūm. But the Mahdī also died the same year. The regime of his successor (*khalīfa*) was weakened by famine and internal strife, which allowed the British to regain control of Sudan in 1898. The family of the Mahdī continues to be involved in Sudanese politics even today.

In Libya, it was the Sanūsiyya (Sanusi) Order that took up the struggle against the Italian invaders in 1911. Founded in 1843 by the mystical sheikh Muḥammad al-Sanūsī (1787–1859), the strictly puritanical order, which – similar to the Arab Wahhābīs – recognized only the Qur'ān and the Sunna as foundations of Islam and frowned upon music and dance, established a number of religious centers (*zāwiya*) and was thus able to expand his influence and economic power from the Sirte and Cyrenaica (East Libya) all the way to central Africa, up to Lake Chad and the Wadai mountains. From its center in the Kufra oases (as of 1895), the order controlled the tribes and peasant inhabitants of a vast area. The Sanusi order tenaciously resisted the French in the Sahara and, starting in 1911, the Italians in Libya. Their resistance remained unbroken into the First World War and the Italians were forced to recognize their state.

Libya's royal house developed after the Second World War from the dynasty of the order sheikhs.

Such religiously inspired resistance movements remained limited to certain regions and, with the exception of the Sanusis and the Arab Wahhābīs, were suppressed by the colonial powers' superior military strength. Towards the end of the nineteenth century, however, pan-Islamic ideas also emerged. Their most important advocate was the enigmatic agitator Jamāl al-Dīn al-Afghānī (ca. 1839–1897). He tried to hide his Iranian, Sh'ite family background behind supposedly Afghani – that is, Sunnī – origins. At the court of the king of Afghanistan, in Cairo and then Istanbul and then back to Cairo (1871–1879), in India, London, and Paris, in Russia, Iraq, and Iran, and finally back to Istanbul, he tirelessly spoke out as a teacher, author, and journalist for a strong, modern Islam that would unite the Muslim peoples in their struggle against the Europeans. He shied away neither from conspiring against Muslim monarchs who were submissive toward Europeans, nor from harshly criticizing the backwardness of the traditional Islamic scholars, the *'ulamā'*. Afghānī inspired an entire generation of Islamic modernists around the turn of the century. His most notable student was the Egyptian Muḥammad 'Abduh (1849–1905). The Islamic legal scholar, who was also a journalist, succeeded in winning the support of the khedive 'Abbās II in 1892 to reform the revered Azhar University, which then introduced modern subjects. In 1899 he became Grand Mufti (chief religious jurist) of Egypt. His Islamic modernism is open to various interpretations. It is invoked today by liberal as well as by Islamist ideologues. *Al-Nahḍa,* the "rebirth" or "renaissance," is the collective term for the movements of the late nineteenth century that proclaimed the revival of an Arabic and an Islamic identity.

Discussion on the future role of Islam in Middle Eastern society also raised the question of the function of the caliphate. The Turkish sultans only began using the title of successor (*khalīfa*) to the Prophet Muḥammad in the eighteenth century. They adopted the title so they could appear before the Russian czar as the patron of his Muslim subjects, since the czar claimed the role of protecting the orthodox Christians in the Balkans. Although the Ottomans were neither members of the Quraysh tribe nor even Arabs at all, they were recognized in Arab countries as the legitimate leaders of the Sunnī *umma*. As the only Muslim state that was still halfway intact, the Ottoman Empire was the obvious political frame of reference for the Sunnī Muslims. At most a kind of Turco-Arabic dual monarchy was considered as a possibility, similar to the Austro-Hungarian Empire – an idea advocated by the secret society of the *Qaḥṭāniyya* (named after the legendary progenitor of the Arabs, see page 25), founded in 1909 by Syrian officers in Constantinople.

The mood began to change after a coup brought the Young Turks to power in Constantinople in 1908. Their regime pursued a course of forced Turkization of the empire. The Turkish language was to take precedence in the army, administration, judiciary, and school instruction; and Arabic was to be repressed. Even the sanctified Arabic call to prayer was to be replaced by a Turkish formula. This Turkish nationalism provoked an Arab nationalism. The idea of the Arab countries' seceding from the Ottoman Empire was raised and the establishment of an Arab caliphate was discussed as well. In 1901 the Syrian ʻAbd ar-Rahmān al-Kawākibī (1849–1903) published a book in Cairo entitled *Umm al-qurā* (The Mother of All Cities) – referring to Mecca – in which he called for the reestablishment of an Arab caliphate. When in 1924 the Turkish national assembly in Ankara declared the caliphate of the Ottoman sultan abolished, scholar and journalist Muḥammad Rashīd Riḍā of Syria (1865–1935) called for the reestablishment of the office of the caliph in his treatise *al-Khilāfa aw al-imāma al-ʻuẓma* (The Caliphate or the Great Imamate). As a follower of Muḥammad ʻAbduh he had immigrated in 1897 to Egypt, where he founded the influential monthly *al-Manār* (The Lighthouse, 1899–1940). Rashīd Riḍā proposed that the holders of the office should be determined by the leading scholars of the entire Islamic world: the scholars of the Azhar in Cairo, the Fatih and Süleymaniye mosques in Istanbul, the Zaytūna Mosque in Tunis, and the religious academy in Deoband, in northern India. One of the most promising candidates for the office was the Sharif of Mecca, al-Ḥusayn ibn ʻAlī (ca. 1853–1931), who had been appointed in 1909 by the Young Turks as "Custodian of the Two Holy Shrines." As a descendant of al-Ḥasan, grandson of the Prophet, he was a member of the Quraysh tribe and the Hāshim clan (see page 29) and therefore also legitimated through religious tradition.

Aside from such pan-Islamic ideas that were rooted in al-Afghānī's agitation, a secular Arab nationalism also became apparent. The question of the existence of an "Arab nation" was posed for the first time in the early twentieth century. In 1869 the Ottoman tanzīmāt reformers proclaimed an "Ottoman" nationality, which included all the countless nationalities of the empire, but the artificial construction was disavowed after 1908 as a result of the Young Turks' crass policies of Turkification and disappeared with the collapse of the empire. Arab nationalisms – at first in plural form – broke new ground. Patriotic clubs and secret societies emerged in major cities such as Damascus and Constantinople, where the future shape of an Arab state was discussed. The framework of considerations remained at first limited to Greater Syria and Mesopotamia as the nucleus and the Arabian peninsula – entirely or in part – as an accessory. Egypt, under British control, remained out of reach. There the notion of an "Egyptian nation" had grown in the nineteenth century; with the territorial isolation of the Nile valley and its five-thousand-year history – first brought into public consciousness by Napoleon's expedition – this was certainly not lacking in historical roots. The Maghreb, however, did not even enter the field of vision at first. There was not yet any talk of a pan-Arab nationalism. A secular Arab nationalism, based on the Arabic language and Arab history and culture, without emphasis on the Muslim religion, appeared attractive especially for the Christian minorities. It is striking that numerous representatives of Arab-nationalist ideologies were Christians.

6

State Building and Independence in the Twentieth Century

Gamal Abdel-Nasser

The First World War and the Mandatory Period

The decision of the Young Turk regime to enter the First World War on the side of the Central Powers sealed the fate of the Ottoman Empire. In response, the Allies abandoned the policy of supporting the "sick man of Europe" and began planning the partition of the empire. In their correspondence from July 1915 to March 1916, the British High Commissioner in Egypt Sir Henry McMahon promised the Sharif of Mecca Ḥusayn ibn 'Alī the crown of an Arabian kingdom in return for fighting against the Turks. From the outset, however, there were disagreements about the borders of this kingdom. According to the Arab position, the northern border was to run about thirty to forty miles north of the current Syrian-Turkish border and include Cilicia with Adana, Tarsus, and the port of Alexandretta (Iskenderun). The British, however, were adamant that predominantly non-Muslim areas such as Mount Lebanon should not be part of the future Arab kingdom. This was to apply for Palestine as well, where, as British Foreign Secretary Arthur Balfour declared on November 2, 1917, "a national home for the Jewish people" was to be established. However, on May 16, 1916, British diplomat Sir Mark Sykes and French Consul General in Beirut François Georges-Picot had already secretly determined their countries' future spheres of influence in the Fertile Crescent.

In the meantime, Sharif Husayn ibn 'Alī and his sons

Faysal and ʻAbdallāh had taken up arms against the Turks in the summer of 1916. On October 29, Husayn ibn ʻAlī assumed the title "King of the Arabs." The British and the French, however, only wanted to recognize him as "King of the Ḥijāz." British Colonel T. E. Lawrence ("Lawrence of Arabia") coordinated attacks on the most important Turkish supply line, the Ḥijāz Railway, and on the Turkish stronghold of al-ʻAqaba, which ended with Husayn triumphantly entering Damascus on October 1, 1918.

The end of the First World War and the Paris peace negotiations raised Arab elites' hopes for imminent independence, in particular since U.S. President Woodrow Wilson had tied the United States' entry into the war with the establishment of the "right to self-determination." As a result, British and French plans to partition the territory could not take place openly. The newly founded League of Nations legitimated their intervention only in the form of preliminary "mandates," which were in fact supposed to prepare those countries for independence.

The Syrian National Congress convened in June 1919 and proclaimed the country's independence on March 7, 1920. The French, however, were not prepared to concede this without a fight. In July 1920, the French defeated the troops of the Sharif's son Faysal and in September secured statehood for Lebanon, that is, the Christian—Maronite-dominated Mount Lebanon, which was expanded to encompass coastal cities, including Beirut, thereby cementing the partition of Lebanon and Syria.

In 1920, Shʻite clerics in Iraq called for a revolt against the British, who had taken power in the country three years earlier. The uprising was quashed in 1921. The British installed Faisal – son of the "King of the Ḥijāz" – as king,

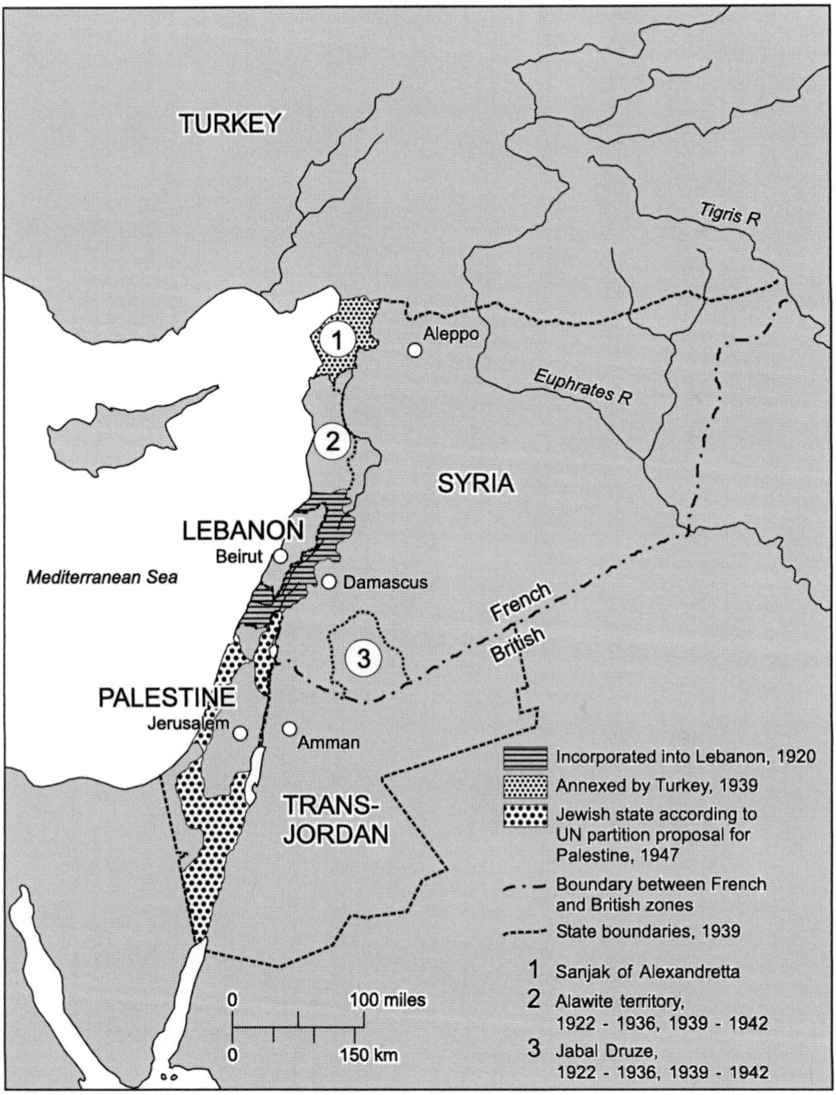

The Anglo-French Levant, 1920–1947

From *The Levant*

while Faisal's brother 'Abdallāh had to content himself with the title "Emir of Transjordan." Jordan became formally independent in 1923, but remained under British mandate. Instead of the hoped-for "Kingdom of the Arabs," the Hashemites were given only three limited territories, two of which remained under British influence. Despite its formal independence, Iraq in particular remained closely tied to British interests through the Anglo-Iraqi treaty of October 1922. The British also retained direct control of Palestine, where the Balfour Declaration – to create a "home for the Jewish people" – was supposed to be implemented. As indicated in a statement by Colonial Minister Winston Churchill, the British were apparently considering a binational state dominated by non-Muslims similar to Maronite-Druze Lebanon. Jewish immigration to Palestine meanwhile continued. In July 1922, the mandate of the League of Nations came into force.

The Hashemites were also the losers on the Arabian Peninsula against the Saudis (*Āl Sa'ūd*) of Najd. In 1902, the young 'Abd al-'Azīz "Ibn Sa'ūd" recaptured Riyadh, thereby initiating the gradual reestablishment of a Saudi-Wahhābīs kingdom. He occupied al-Hasā, the eastern province of the Ottoman Empire on the Persian Gulf, in 1912, and conquered 'Asīr, the mountainous landscape south of Mecca, in 1920. Although al-'Azīz was initially forced to recognize Ottoman suzerainty and content himself with the title of provincial governor in 1914, the titles he assumed illustrate his inexorable rise. In 1915 he declared himself "Emir of Najd," and in 1921, "Sultan of Najd and Its Dependencies." His political power was based on the military settlements he had established in 1913, which were comprised of Bedouin tribes he had settled and won over to Wahhabism and that formed a secret religious fraternal organization known as *al-Ikhwān* or "the Brotherhood," which he used in battle whenever necessary. After the Turkish National Assembly in Ankara declared the caliphate of the Ottoman sultan abolished in March 1924, a conflict emerged with the Sharif of Mecca Ḥusayn ibn 'Alī. The Sharif assumed the title of caliph, in response to which Ibn Sa'ūd sent his Ikhwān to Mecca, which he entered in December 1924. On January 8, 1926, Ibn Sa'ūd had himself declared "King of the Ḥijāz and Sultan of Najd." The British recognized Ibn Sa'ūd's independence in 1927, and his state was officially named "The Kingdom of Saudi Arabia" in 1932.

Zaghlūl Pasha (Sa'd Zaghlūl), a graduate of Azhar University and a lawyer by profession, led the struggle for independence in Egypt. He was the leader of a delegation (*wafd*) to London that sought unsuccessfully to negotiate the abrogation of protectorate status. The delegation also traveled to the Paris Peace Conference but there as well efforts remained fruitless. Zaghlūl's arrest and exile triggered rioting in Egypt that ultimately led the British to end the protectorate status, which was officially abolished in 1922. Egypt became a constitutional monarchy in 1923. Khedive Ismā'īl's son was crowned King Fu'ād I, but the British retained military control over the country. Until his death in 1927, Sa'd Zaghlūl, head of the Wafd party and briefly Prime Minister, sought to limit the king's autocracy. In 1936, an Anglo-Egyptian treaty regulated the rights of the former protectorate power and continued to allow British troops to be stationed at the Suez Canal.

The Salafiyya and the Muslim Brotherhood

Like its rival the *Wafd* party, the Muslim Brotherhood (*al-Ikhwān al-muslimūn*) in Egypt opposed the royal court and its politics. The brotherhood was founded in 1928 by Hasan al-Bannā (1906–1949), a primary school teacher who had belonged to various religious associations before establishing the brotherhood. With Bannā as "Supreme Guide" (*al-murshid al-'āmm*), the Muslim Brotherhood was organized according to a strict discipline. Modeled on mystic Sufi orders of the past, it developed into a modern mass movement with about half a million members in Egypt after the Second World War and numerous offshoots in the mandate territories. The goal of the organization was a total "Islamic order" (*al-niẓām al-islāmī*), that is, a political, social, and economic order based exclusively on the Qur'ān and the Sunna. The details of this order remained vague, as al-Bannā's missives and journal contributions were rather abstract, as were the principles established at a general conference held in Cairo in 1939. While the basic precept was undisputed, namely, that the traditional Islamic legal order of the Sharī'a should be reintroduced, it remained unclear what form this uncodified – and in principle uncodifiable – order should take.

The Muslim Brotherhood is the oldest and most successful of the various modern organizations that force Islam into an ideological corset and a self-sufficient organizational form for the purpose of achieving political and, above all, social aims and that can be designated as "Islamism" – as it is a modern ideology – in distinction to traditional Islam. The Muslim Brotherhood was the heir to those intellectuals who founded the Salafiyya movement around the turn of the century, an ideology that propagated an idealized conception of an original Islam, the golden era of "the pious predecessors" (*al-salaf al-ṣāliḥ*) – that is, the Prophet Muhammad, his first four successors, and their companions – as a model for the present. In particular the publicist Rashīd Riḍā (see page 140) can be seen as a pioneer of this idea. Islam as a total system regulating all domains of life "is at once a religion and a state order" (*al-Islām dīn wa-dawla*). While this ideological postulate largely ignores the facts of Islamic history, it has nevertheless proved extremely effective as a slogan: "Islam is the solution" (*al-Islām al-ḥall*) to all political and social problems. Like the founders of the Muslim Brotherhood, the supporters of the movement have largely been members of the middle class and farmers, groups on whose behalf the organization has intervened when the state lacked either the will or the means. The brotherhood seeks to provide food and education as well as a technical infrastructure for the rapidly growing and barely urbanized populace in larger cities. After a member of the Muslim Brotherhood assassinated Egyptian prime minister Nuqrāshī Pasha in 1948, the movement was banned and went underground. Ḥasan al-Bannā was killed by the political police in 1949.

The Palestine Question

The British Balfour Declaration, which affirmed "the establishment in Palestine of a national home for the Jewish people," remained unfulfilled even a number of years after the First World War. Many Arabs were alarmed by increased Jewish immigration. Between 1932 and 1935, the Jewish population in Palestine rose from seventeen to twenty-seven percent. There had already been repeated riots and clashes in the 1920s. The polemic became increasingly heated and assumed religious tones. In 1933, Rashīd Ridā declared that anyone who sold land to the British or to Jews was a traitor to Islam, and in 1935, the Mufti of Jerusalem Amīn al-Husaynī issued a *fatwa* or legal pronouncement, which, in a free interpretation of the Quran verse 33:72, designated Palestine as the "possession (*amāna*)" divinely entrusted to Muslims. The Nazi persecution of Jews and the global depression contributed to increasing Jewish immigration and an intensification of the conflict. Militant groups formed. The first revolt of Palestinian Arabs against the British mandate began in 1936 and ended when the Second World War started in 1939. In 1937, the British Peel Commission presented a partition plan that sought to limit the future Jewish state to Galilee and the coastal area down to south of Tel Aviv with Jerusalem and the port of Jaffa remaining part of the mandate territory. There were Arab conferences on Palestine in 1931 and 1937 addressing the future of the country, but neither was able to achieve any palpable success.

The Second World War and the Establishment of the Arab League

Many Arabs sympathized with the Axis powers during the Second World War. This was due in part to the enmity Arabs felt toward Great Britain and France as colonial powers as well as to concerns about continued Jewish immigration to Palestine. Fascist organizations arose sporadically, and anti-Semitic currents – in fact foreign to traditional Islam – also became evident. The British curbed Jewish immigration in 1939, and in May 1941 Foreign Secretary Anthony Eden even declared his support for future Arab unity. However, de Gaulle's government in exile granted independence to Lebanon in 1943 and to Syria in 1945, thus sealing the permanence of their partition. For the duration of the war, France and England retained their control of Arab countries.

The impending Allied victory raised the possibility of independence for the remaining Arab countries as well as issues of Arab unity, especially that of Palestine's place in the Arab world. For this reason, increased preparations for liberation were made even during the war. After preparatory negotiations in Alexandria in 1944, Egypt, Transjordan, Lebanon, Syria, Iraq, and Saudi Arabia, all of which were already formally independent, approved the Pact of the League of Arab States in Cairo on March 22, 1945. (North)

Yemen joined on May 5, and the charter came into force on May 11. The goal of the pact was to promote economic, cultural, and social cooperation among Arab countries. It obligated all members to a foreign policy that did not contravene the interests of other member states and that affirmed the right of Arabs to Palestine.

Membership in the Arab League

1945	Egypt, Jordan, Lebanon, Syria, Iraq, Yemen, Saudi Arabia	1971	Bahrain, Qatar, United Arab Emirates, Oman
1953	Libya	1973	Mauritania
1956	Sudan	1974	Somalia
1958	Tunisia, Morocco	1976	Palestine (represented by the PLO)
1961	Kuwait	1977	Djibouti
1962	Algeria	1993	Comoros
1967	South Yemen		

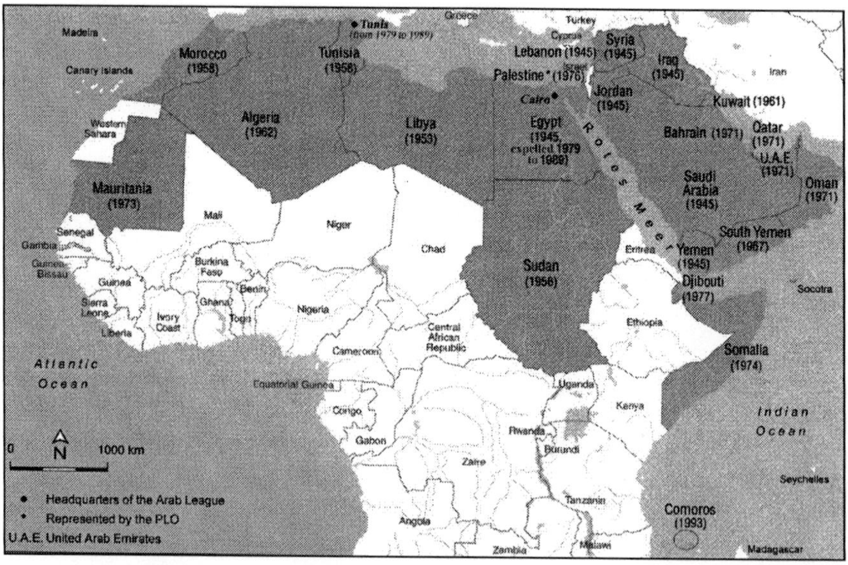

The member states of the Arab League with their year of entry.

The Founding of Israel and the First Middle East War

In 1947, the United Nations presented a partition plan for the future of Palestine. Arab states, however, refused to recognize this plan and voted against it at the UN General Assembly. Consequently, Great Britain announced that at midnight on May 15, 1948, it was abandoning its mandate for Palestine. In Tel Aviv on May 14, 1948, David Ben-Gurion proclaimed the state of Israel. Troops from member states of the Arab League responded by advancing on the following night. This intervention by Arab allies, who were poorly organized both militarily and politically, ended in a debacle. When a ceasefire was declared on January 7, 1949, Israel had made territorial gains considerably beyond the UN partition plan. The ceasefire line, which in Jerusalem ran directly west of the city wall in the old city, remained the de facto border between the Jewish state and its Arab neighbors for almost twenty years. The West Bank with East Jerusalem went to Jordan, while the Gaza Strip went to Egypt.

The catastrophe (*al-nakba*) was enormous. Flight and expulsion (about sixty percent of the 1.4 million Arab residents of the former mandate territory emigrated), dispossession, and the destruction of more than four hundred Arab villages by Jewish settlers laid the foundation for a conflict that continues even today and to which no end is in sight. There is no political development, no conflict in the Middle East that is not in some way affected by the Palestine conflict.

Ba'th Party and Nasserism

The major ideologies of the nineteenth and twentieth centuries – liberalism, socialism, communism, and fascism – all had their supporters in the Arab world as well. Following the Second World War, Arab nationalism, which had previously assumed a more regional form ("Egypt for Egyptians"), took on pan-Arab tones. The establishment of the Arab League indicated the direction of future developments. People spoke of a single "Arab nation," defined in particular through a common language, history, and culture, and no longer through Islam. It was above all Christian authors from Syria and Lebanon who laid the theoretical foundations for secular Arab nationalism (Pan-Arabism). This is evident, for example, in the fact that in 1940 two Syrian teachers, the Christian Michel 'Aflaq and the Muslim Salāḥ al-Dīn al-Bītār, founded the *Ba'th* ("resurrection" or "renaissance"), a socialist party opposing the power of the wealthy bourgeoisie and large landowners. It did not take long before additional leftist nationalist groups merged with the party. The declared goals of the Ba'th were Arab "unity, freedom, and socialism." The party was oriented around a secular nationalist ideology, in which Islam was regarded as merely one part of a common cultural Arab heritage.

While the Maghreb states initially remained under French rule, there was a series of revolutions in the eastern part of the Arab world directed against the ruling elite: the land-owning class (which had arisen in the nineteenth century), the wealthy bourgeoisie, and the established dynasties. These revolutions were triggered above all by unresolved social problems, as well as by the failure of old elites with regard to the Palestine issue and their collaboration with the former colonial powers (which continued to exert influence in the area). Leaders of the revolutionary movements were frequently officers, who themselves came from the middle classes and found support there.

A series of military coups began in Syria in 1949, resulting in successive military dictatorships. However, the actual decade of revolts occurred between 1952 and 1962. It was during this period that the remaining Arab countries obtained their independence. In Egypt, the "Free Officers," including Gamāl 'Abd al-Nāṣir (Nasser, 1918–1970), brought down the regime of King Fārūq (1936–1952) in 1952. In Syria, after the parliamentary system was reinstituted in 1954, the Ba'th had their first great election victory. The party was the driving force behind the experimental unification with Egypt (see page 158). In the same year, a long guerrilla war against the French began in Algeria. By 1962, approximately 20,000 French and 1,000,000 Algerians had lost their lives in the conflict. The Algerian independence struggle mobilized people far beyond Algeria and the Arab world. It came to be seen as the paradigm for liberation movements throughout the Third World. The "Independence" party (*Istiqlāl*) was founded in Morocco in 1944. The popular Sultan Muḥammad V (1927–1958) led the national movement. The French exiled him to Madagascar in 1953, but due to the rioting in the country they were forced to bring him back, and granted Morocco full independence on March 2, 1956. On that same day, Habib Bourguiba (*Bū Ruqaiba*), a lawyer, assumed leadership of the New Constitutional Party (Neo–Destour, see page 132) in Tunisia. In Iraq, King ʻAbdallāh was deposed and murdered in a putsch by Colonel Qassim (*al-Qāsim*). In Yemen, there was a coup by the army against the Zaydī imam al-Badr in 1962; the proclamation of a republic led to a civil war that lasted eight years. Last to fall was the monarchy in Libya. Here young officers, led by Colonel Muʻammar al-Qaddafi (born in 1942), deposed King Idrīs from the dynasty of the Sanusi sheikhs in 1969. In the same year, the military led by Colonel Jaʻfar Numayrī assumed power in Sudan.

During Nasser's presidency (1954–1970), Egypt assumed the leading political role in the Arab world. Nasser was successful in a number of actions that greatly enhanced his prestige, even far beyond Egypt's borders. The first of these was his treaty with the British in 1954 regarding the definitive withdrawal of their troops. The nationalization of the Suez Canal in July 1956 did lead to the final military intervention by France and Great Britain in alliance with Israel in October and November of that year, but this was brought to a halt by the two superpowers, the United States and the Soviet Union. On February 1, 1958, Nasser announced that the Syrian Baʻth Party had agreed to a union between Egypt and Syria as the "United Arab Republic" (UAR), which Yemen – at the time still governed by the imam – formally entered. This union was supposed to be the seed of a united Arab nation. A joint National Assembly was formed in 1960. Only a year later, however, the Syrians, who felt dominated by the Egyptians, withdrew from the union following a rightist coup. When revolutionary officers in Yemen brought down the imam in 1962 and proclaimed a republic, Nasser took their side and supported the revolutionaries in the subsequent civil war from 1962 to 1969, especially with his air force.

The United States sought to contain the Soviet Union and keep it out of the Indian Ocean and away from Middle Eastern oil reserves by means of the Baghdad Pact of 1955 (between Turkey, Iraq, Iran, and Pakistan), the Middle East Treaty Organization orchestrated by Britain and the United States. Nasser initially attempted to lead the Non-Aligned Movement, but then increasingly sought support from the Eastern bloc, which helped to finance the new enormous Aswan High Dam. Iraq, Syria, Libya, Algeria, Somalia, and South Yemen (which became independent in 1967) all relied on support from the Soviet Union and on intimate economic, military, and political cooperation with the Eastern bloc.

The Six-Day War (June 1967)

Nasser's star began to wane when he overestimated his own power and engaged in a war with Israel to liberate all of Palestine. Palestinian exiles in Kuwait – including Yasir Arafat (1929-2004) – founded the Fataḥ Organization (*al-Fatḥ*, "the victory") in 1959. In January 1965, the organization called for an armed struggle against Israel. The Syrian Ba'th party's support of the Fataḥ Organization led Nasser to worry about his reputation as leader of the Arab nation; although inadequately armed he took the reins of a movement that threatened to slip out of his control. He provoked a war by occupying the Sinai Peninsula and demanding the withdrawal of UN troops. Like the war of 1948–1949, the Six-Day War (June 5–10, 1967) ended in a military disaster for the Arab side. Israel took not only East Jerusalem (the old city), which had been in Jordanian control, but also the entire West Bank and the Gaza Strip, where a Jewish settlement policy was introduced that has subsequently been supported or tolerated by all Israeli governments.

This defeat marked the demise of Nasserism, the failure of an ideology of nationalist, pan-Arabist, and socialist ideas. Nasser's death in 1970 bolstered Islamic movements and groups throughout the world.

The Sadat Era (1970–1981) The October War, the Infitāḥ, and the Oil Crisis

In 1971, Egyptians approved the new liberal constitution (which nonetheless granted the president extensive powers) presented by Nasser's successor Anwar al-Sadat (al-Sādāt). In October 1973, Sadat sent troops across the Suez Canal in a surprise attack, though the victory was quickly neutralized by the United States' intervention. Nevertheless, Egypt regained the Sinai, and the Suez Canal was opened again in 1975. Sadat paid for this partial success by turning to the West politically, ending Egypt's socialist experiment, and liberalizing the economy, in short, by "opening" (*infitāḥ*) the country to Western capital. In 1977, Sadat made a surprise trip to Israel, prayed in the Aqsa Mosque, and spoke before the Knesset. On March 26, 1979, Egypt became the first Arab country reach a peace agreement with Israel at the U.S. Camp David, which included the recognition of their shared border. A "rejectionist front" formed by other Arab countries opposed the peace agreement, and Egypt's membership in the Arab League was suspended from 1979 to 1989.

One consequence of the October War of 1973 – known as the Yom Kippur War in Israel and the Ramadān War among Arabs – was the so-called oil price revolution. The founding of the Organization of Petroleum Exporting Countries (OPEC) in 1960 marked an attempt to counter-balance the power of multinational oil companies. The oil embargo of 1973-74, which was agreed to in Vienna as a political weapon, led to unparalleled price increases: The cost of a barrel of oil increased tenfold. This led to an unprecedented flow of capital into the oil exporting countries, particularly Saudi Arabia. The oil embargo was not successful in terms of foreign policy, as consumer nations were able to turn to their own resources to reduce consumption and to develop alternative energy sources. In terms of domestic politics, this influx of capital did more to cement existing political structures than to change them. Saudi Arabia, as a distributor of petrodollars, was now able to exercise a certain hegemony over the other Arab countries, especially those without oil reserves and those bordering on Israel. The Saudis used their influence to strengthen Islamist movements, first and foremost the Muslim Brotherhood, as well as regional tribal leaders, for example in (North) Yemen and South Yemen, thereby weakening leftist revolutionary movements and parties.

The Islamic revolution in Iran in 1978–79 toppled the pro-American regime of the Shah and led to the establishment of the Islamic Republic of Iran under Āyatollāh Khomeinī. It also fueled the hopes of Arab Islamists that similar coups would be possible in their own countries. On November 20, 1979, a group of approximately five hundred Saudi sectarians proclaiming the return of the awaited Mahdi occupied Islam's most sacred shrine, the Masjid al-Harām mosque with the Ka'ba in Mecca. Authorities were able to overpower them only after a two-week siege. The murder of Sadat during a parade in Cairo on October 6, 1981, was also the work of militant Islamists from Upper Egypt. Between 1983 and 1985, Sudanese dictator Colonel Nimeiry, who was supported by the Muslim Brotherhood, experimented with implementing Islamic law, introducing penal and tax codes based on the Sharī'a.

The Lebanese Civil War (1975–1990) and the Iran-Iraq War (1980–1988)

For the regimes of most Arab countries, the 1970s, 1980s, and 1990s proved to be a period of unprecedented stability. In July 1968, the Iraqi Ba'th party led by General Aḥmad Ḥasan al-Bakr ousted President 'Ārif in a bloodless coup and assumed control of the country for the next thirty-five years. Colonel Qaddafi came to power in Libya in 1969 after bringing down the monarchy and continues to rule the country even today. In 1970, then Syrian minister of defense Ḥāfiz al-Asad participated in a coup and established a Ba'thist regime, which his son Bashar has continued after Asad's death in 2000. The assassination of leading politicians did not affect this stability. In Egypt the transition from Sadat to President Ḥusnī Mubārak (born in 1928) in 1981 brought no fundamental political changes. The murder of King Faisal in 1975 shook the Saudi monarchy as little as did the transition from his successor Khālid to King Fahd in 1982. The Hashemite king Hussain ruled Jordan from 1952 to 1999, King Ḥasan II ruled in Morocco from 1961 to 1999, and Sultan Qābūs has governed Oman since 1970. The FLN (*Front de libération nationale*), which led Algeria's war for independence against France and came to power after independence was achieved in 1962, has also successfully cemented its power. Habib Bourguiba, who had ruled Tunisia after independence in 1956, was removed in 1987 by the former prime minister General Zīn El-ʻĀbidīne Ben ʻAlī (born in 1936), a change of power that also took place within the ruling elite.

This stability was attained almost universally by the cementing of existing power relations and the rigorous use of police and secret service. In Syria, President al-Asad violently suppressed the opposition of the Muslim Brotherhood. More than 10,000 people are said to have died in the bombing of the city of Ḥamāh. The governments of Egypt, Jordan, and Morocco have, in contrast, attempted to integrate the Islamist opposition through concessions and limited, controlled government participation.

Despite their nationalist, pan-Arabist ideology, the Baʻth regimes in Syria and Iraq had only narrow regional power bases. Hafīz al-Asad was supported especially by the Alawites, a small Shʻite religious community in the Syrian coastal range (not to be confused with the Alevis in Turkey). Many Alawite men have made a career in the Syrian military, particularly in the air force. Saddam Hussein (born in 1937), who took control of the Iraqi Baʻth party in 1979, ruled the country with the help of the Tikrīt clan, a circle loyal to him with its roots in and around Tikrīt, Saddam's native city on the Tigris. This regional and narrowly limited power base and a political agenda organized primarily around securing its own rule have made both Baʻth regimes completely incapable of effectively representing pan-Arab interests and have also brought them into open rivalry with each other more than once.

Lebanon, in contrast, has been unstable. An unwritten "national pact" has existed here since independence in

1943, regulating the separation of power in the legislative and executive branches according to precisely balanced percentages of the different religious groups. It gave Christians, especially the Maronites, political advantage over Druzes, Sh'ites, and Sunnīs. However, consensus on this proportionality disintegrated in the 1970s as a result of demographic displacements caused primarily by the influx of Palestinians, as well as growth in the Sh'ite population in southern Lebanon. As the government had lost virtually all control over the south of the country, fighters of the Palestinian Liberation Organization (PLO), founded in 1964 in response to the defeat in the Six-Day War, were able to settle here among the primarily Sh'ite population after being driven out of the West Bank, establishing training camps and engaging in attacks on villages on the Israeli side of the border.

Open civil war erupted in Lebanon in 1975. The PLO was the spearhead for the Muslim minorities here, who sought to break the Christian dominance that had been firmly established since the nineteenth century. The Syrian military intervened on the side of the Muslims, an action that the Arab League then legitimated through a retrospective mandate in the summer of 1976. After the Islamic Revolution in Iran in 1979, the Sh'ites in southern Lebanon became increasingly radicalized. Their militant organization Hezbollah (*Hizbu'llāh*, "party of God") joined in the struggle against Israel. This led to a military intervention by Israel in 1982–83, which ended with the occupation of Beirut, a renewed but brief invigoration of Christian forces, and the expulsion of the PLO from southern Lebanon. PLO leader Yasir Arafat went into exile in Tunisia. The general exhaustion of the embattled militias prepared the way for negotiations, which led to a peace plan under the aegis of the Arab League in Ṭā'if, Saudi Arabia in the fall of 1989. The plan was supposed to end the civil war and establish a new political basis in the country. At the end of 1990, the Ṭā'if Agreement was enforced by Syrian troops (who have remained in the country) and written into the constitution.

After the Islamic Revolution led to a regime change in Iran in 1979, Iraqi president Saddam Hussein believed that he could now assert Iraq's old claims to the mouth of the Shatt al-'Arab (the confluence of the Tigris and Euphrates rivers) and to the Iranian border province of Khūzestān, an area rich in oil with a predominantly Arab population. For the United States and its Western allies, Saddam's war against the new Iranian regime offered a welcome opportunity to retaliate against an enemy that had subverted an important pillar of American alliance building in the Middle East, and they provided the Iraqis with support. This war in the Persian Gulf region lasted eight years (1980–1988) and ended in a stalemate. Initially pushed back by Iranian troops, the Iraqis were subsequently able to regain territory. When the Iranian leader Khomeinī was forced to accept a ceasefire, the prewar borders at Shatt al-'Arab were reestablished.

The 1990's: The First Intifāḍa and the Gulf War

Mikhail Gorbachev's policy of perestroika beginning in 1986 and the collapse of the Soviet Union in 1990 marked the dissolution of antagonisms between the Soviet Union and the United States. The Cold War had allowed the Arab states to seek support from one superpower or the other according to their needs. The United States was now the sole superpower that Arab governments had to come to terms with.

The end of the opposition between East and West also rendered Palestine superfluous as a substitute battleground for the superpowers. It was now possible for the United States and the Soviet Union to work together for a solution to the conflict in the West Bank and the Gaza Strip. There had been strikes and heavy rioting in these areas in late 1987. This first *Intifāḍa* ("uprising") continued throughout 1988 and 1989. The central committee of the PLO, which was still in exile in Tunis, declared Yasir Arafat president of an "Independent State of Palestine." Israel took part in top-secret talks with the PLO in Oslo, and official negotiations were held under the aegis of the United States and the Soviet Union in Madrid in October 1991. These negotiations were facilitated by the election of the Labor Party in Israel and the formation of Yitzhak Rabin's government in the summer of 1992. A limited autonomy on the basis of the formula "Land for Peace" was ultimately negotiated on

August 19, 1993. Initially for Gaza and Jericho, it was supposed to be gradually expanded. Israel and the PLO agreed to recognize each other. The agreement, which was signed in Washington in the presence of President Bill Clinton on September 13, 1993, appeared finally to provide the foundation for lasting peace in the Middle East. Arafat, Prime Minister Rabin, and Foreign Minister Shimon Peres were awarded the Nobel Peace Prize in 1994.

In the meantime, however, U.S. involvement in the Middle East had acquired a new dimension when, in August 1990, Saddam Hussein occupied Kuwait and claimed its oil reserves as compensation for his expenditures in the Iran-Iraq War. The independent country of Kuwait, a member state of the United Nations, was proclaimed a province that had historically belonged to Iraq. Saddam hoped that in alliance with Syria and Yemen he could break Saudi Arabia's hegemony and gain access to oil reserves along the Persian Gulf. However, if Saddam had thought that the United States would tacitly support or tolerate this move, he was grievously mistaken. Supported by a United Nations resolution, the United States forged an alliance of twenty-eight nations, including most Arab countries, even Syria. Only Libya, Jordan, and the PLO sided with Iraq. After the ultimatum expired in January 1991, American and allied troops defeated the Iraqi army in the fourteen-day operation called Desert Storm, which was launched from Saudi territory. Coalition forces, however, neither advanced to Baghdad nor toppled the Ba'th regime. Saddam Hussein was even able to violently suppress a Sh'ite uprising in the south of the country in 1991 and to retaliate with mass executions without any reaction by the victors. The economic sanctions imposed by the United Nations have seriously damaged the economic infrastructure of the country and hit the civilian population the hardest. The victors also erected no-fly zones north of the 36th parallel and south of the 33rd parallel in order to protect the Kurds and the Sh'ites from further reprisals. Iraq's constant obstruction of UN weapon inspectors, who were supposed to prevent Iraqi production of nuclear, biological, and chemical weapons, soon brought Saddam Hussein into renewed conflict with the United States.

7

The Beginning of the Twenty-first Century

Baghdad 2006

The Second Intifāḍa

In the summer of 2000, talks between the PLO and the Israeli government of Ehud Barak resumed under the aegis of the United States, nourishing hopes for a final peace in the Israel-Palestine conflict. But Camp David II was an utter failure, especially – although details were never officially made public – regarding the issues of the fixing of the border, the problematic right of return for displaced Palestinians, and the question of Jerusalem. The Arab enclaves in East Jerusalem would have remained separated from the Palestinian state and interspersed with Jewish settlements. On the Ḥaram al-Sharīf – the Temple Mount of the Jews – the Palestinians would have had owned the al-Aqṣā Mosque and the Dome of the Rock, but not the ground on which they stood. Yasir Arafat rejected Barak's offer as unacceptable for the Palestinians. Then the provocative appearance on the Temple Mount by Ariel Sharon, then right-wing leader of the opposition, on September 28, 2000, triggered the Second Intifāḍa, which led to an extraordinary escalation of the conflict, with a series of suicide attacks by the radical Islamist Palestinian organizations *al-Jihād al-islāmi* and *Ḥamās* ("enthusiasm, zeal"; actually an acronym for Islamic Resistance Movement) and military reprisals by Israel, during which 'Arafāt was temporarily besieged in his headquarters in Ramallāh. The "road map" proposed in 2003 by U.S. president George W. Bush in cooperation with the United Nations, the European Union, and Russia, which

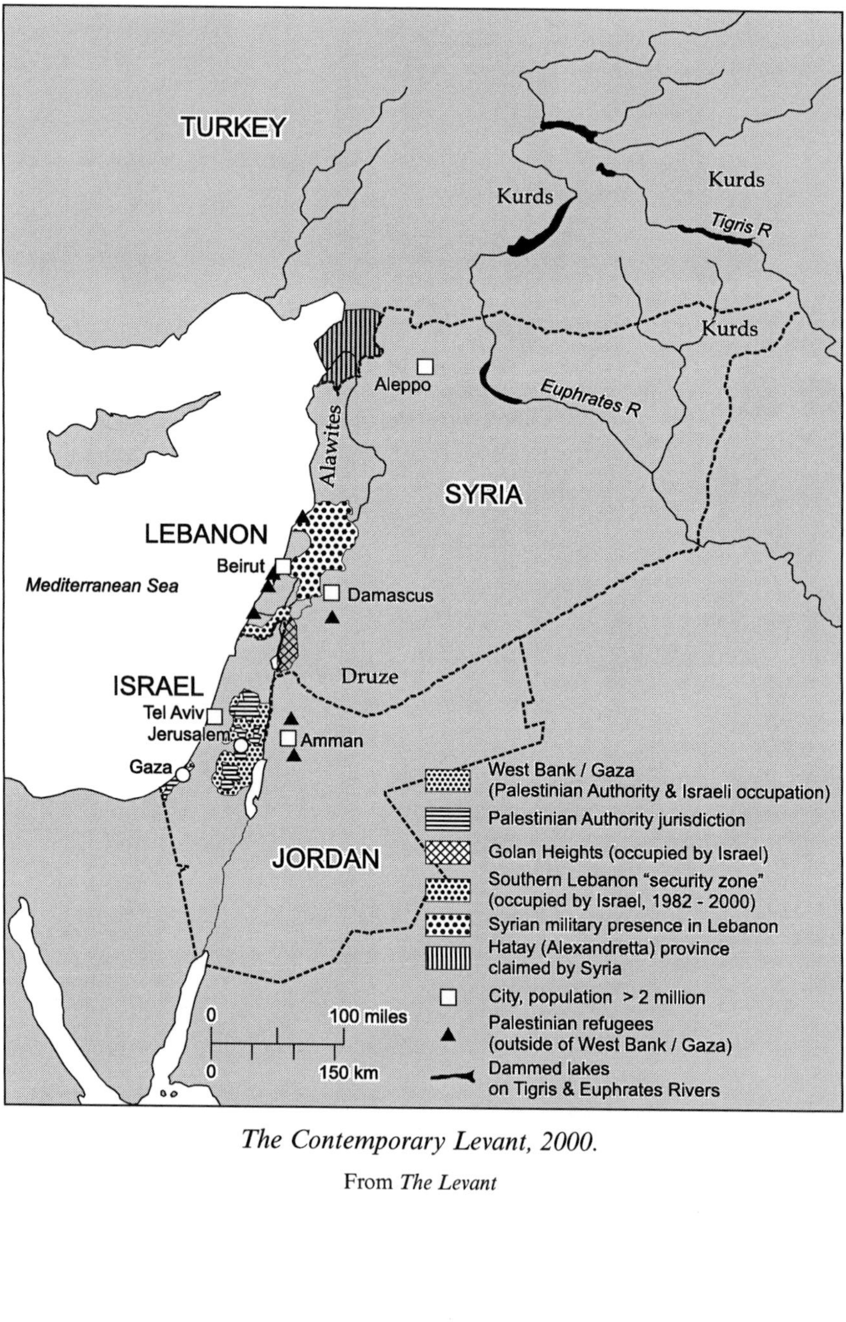

The Contemporary Levant, 2000.

From *The Levant*

was intended to lead to a final peace, was quickly removed from the negotiating table. Even though the Jewish settlements in the Gaza Strip have been removed, the resolution of the conflict seems more distant than ever. The electoral victory of the radical Islamist Ḥamās in the Palestinian territories and the Israeli army's attack on the positions of the Hezbollah militias (Sh'ites supported by Iran) in southern Lebanon in the summer of 2006 have dangerously intensified the situation.

The Iraq War

The attacks on the World Trade Center and the Pentagon on September 11, 2001, by nineteen assassins of Arab descent led to a provisional reorientation of U.S. Middle East policies, the ultimate effects of which remain to be seen. A second military intervention in Iraq was part of considerations by the U.S. government from the very beginning. Various justifications were offered for attacking Saddam Hussein's Ba'th regime: Saddam's alleged production of weapons of mass destruction; support for the terrorist organization Al-Qā'ida ("the basis") of Usāma bin Lādin, which was responsible for the attacks of September 11; and regime change in Iraq to start the process of democratization in the entire region. Only the last of these carries any real weight. The U.S. government evidently planned to restructure the entire region. The attack by U.S. and British units, this time from bases in Kuwait, started on March 20, 2003, and toppled Saddam Hussein's regime with the capture of Baghdad on April 9. Saddam himself managed to escape, but was apprehended on December 13. Many senior officials were arrested or turned themselves in. Civil authority was initially placed under American civilian administration, which was responsible for the country's reconstruction. The armies of the victors, meanwhile reinforced by Poland and other allies, remained in the country.

Whether or not Iraq can be pacified is largely dependent on the position of the Sh'ite population, which makes up about sixty-five percent of the total Iraqi population. If the autonomous Kurds are not included in these statistics, then the Sh'ites comprise seventy-five percent of the Arab population, compared to twenty-five percent Arab Sunnīs. Even in the capital of Baghdad, which lies within the so-called Sunnī Triangle, the Sh'ites have probably long since become a majority of the population. The influx of refugees from the south following the Iran-Iraq War of 1980–88 have transformed the suburbs of al-Kāzimiyya in the north, with its Sh'ite shrine, and the former Saddam City in the east (now named Sadr City, *Madīnat al-Ṣadr,* after a Sh'ite Āyatollāh murdered at the behest of Saddam), with their two to three million residents, into Sh'ite strongholds. These could play a significant role in a conflict for power in the future Iraq. Although Āyatollāh as-Sīstānī, leading cleric of the Sh'ite university complex in Najaf, supports nonviolent resistance in the time-honored quietist tradition of senior Sh'ite clergy – in contrast to the young Muqtadā as-Ṣadr, who organizes armed militias in Sadr City – the Sh'ites oppose foreign occupation forces in general, which coincides with the Sunnī opposition. A national resistance in which Arab identity carries more weight than religious affiliation is starting to form. Any order imposed on the people from the outside without their approval would remain unstable. But no matter how the experiment ends, the occupation and subjugation of a major Arab country by the United States has opened up a completely new chapter in the history of the Arabs.

The Arab countries between the Atlantic and the Tigris are today considered part of the "crisis belt," which extends even farther to include Iran, Afghanistan, and the Indian subcontinent, all the way to southeast Asia. The centers of conflict in this part of the world are indeed numerous. Violent coups, wars, and civil wars have followed one after another since the end of the Second World War. The perpetual conflict around Palestine seems far from resolution. Again and again, oil reserves in several Arab countries provide grounds for foreign powers to intervene politically or militarily in pursuit of their own interests. And let us not forget that for a period of time the entire Arab world, with the exception of central Arabia, was subject to more or less direct European colonial rule; that is a trauma that still has enormous aftereffects today and continues to feed anti-Western attitudes. Especially the foundation of Israel, a state of European emigrants, is viewed within this context as a source of outrage as long as the Palestinians are not allowed to have their own country. On top of this are the immense demographic and economic problems and the unresolved questions of the future political order. The models of the dictatorial or patrimonial regimes and the traditional monarchies that have prevailed until now are competing with the ideas of democratic constitutions and with drafts for Islamist state and social systems, as favored by the Muslim Brotherhood. The Arab countries have meanwhile become fully integrated into the framework of the global economy and world politics. Their internal policies will have to adapt to that. It remains to be seen from which political elites change might be forthcoming.

Bibliography

GENERAL WORKS

Ulrich Haarmann and Heinz Halm, eds., *Geschichte der arabischen Welt,* 4th revised and expanded edition (Munich: C.H. Beck, 2001).

Albert Hourani, *A History of the Arab Peoples* (New York: Warner Books, 1992).

Bernard Lewis, *The Arabs in History,* 6th ed. (Oxford and New York: Oxford Univ. Press, 1993 [first ed.: London and New York: Hutchinson's University Library, 1950]).

PRE-ISLAMIC ARABIA

G. W. Bowersock, *Roman Arabia,* (Cambridge, Mass.: Harvard Univ. Press, 1983).

Jan Retsō, *The Arabs in Antiquity: Their History from the Assyrians to the Umayyads,* (London and New York: Routledge Curzon, 2003).

THE BEGINNINGS OF ISLAM

Hartmut Bobzin, *Mohammed,* 3rd ed. (Munich: C.H. Beck, 2006 [2000]).

———, *Der Koran* (Munich: C.H. Beck, 1999).

Fred McGraw Donner, *The Early Muslim Conquests,* (Princeton: Princeton Univ. Press, 1981).

Hugh Kennedy, *The Early 'Abbaāsid Caliphate: A Political History,* (Totowa, NJ: Barnes and Noble, 1981).

Rudi Paret, *Mohammed und der Koran,* (Stuttgart: W. Kohlhammer, 1957) (reprinted numerous times).

———, *Der Koran,* (Stuttgart: W. Kohlhammer Verlag:1999).

Montgomery Watt, *Muhammad at Mecca,* (Oxford: Clarendon Press, 1953).

———, *Muhammad at Medina,* (Oxford: Clarendon Press, 1956).

Julius Wellhausen, *The Arab Kingdom and Its Fall,* trans. Margaret Graham Weir (Beirut: Khayats, 1963 [first English ed.: Calcutta: Univ. of Calcutta, 1927]).

'ARABIYYA

Johann Fūck, *Arabiya. Untersuchungen zur arabischen Sprach- und Stilgeschichte,* (Berlin: Akademischer Verlag, 1950).

Hamilton A. R. Gibb, *Arabic Literature: An Introduction* (Oxford and New York: Oxford Univ. Press, 1962)}.

Wolfhart Heinrichs, *Neues Handbuch der Literaturwissenschaft,*vol. 5: *Orientalisches Mittelalter,* Wiebelsheim: Aula Verlag, 1990).

Charles Pellat, *The Life and Works of Jāhiz,* translation of selected texts, trans. D. M. Hawke (London: Routledge & K. Paul, 1969).

ARAB RECEPTION OF ANTIQUITY

Dimitri Gutas, *Greek Thought, Arabic Culture: The Graeco-Arabic Translation Movement in Baghdad and Early 'Abbaāsid Society (2nd–4th, 8th–10th centuries*), (London and New York: Routledge, 1981).

Franz Rosenthal, *Das Fortleben der Antike im Islam,* (Zurich: Artemis, 1965).

Gotthard Strohmaier, *Von Demokrit bis Dante. Die Bewahrung antiken Erbes in der arabischen Kultur* (Hildesheim, Zurich, and New York: Georg Olms, 1996) (*Olms Studien* 43).

Juan Vernet, *La Cultura hispano ărabe en Oriente y Occidente* (Barcelona: Ariel Historia, 1978).

THE MAMLUKS

David Ayalon, *The Mamluk Military Society,* (London: Variorum Reprints, 1979).

Daniel Pipes, *Slave Soldiers and Islam: The Genesis of a Military System,* (New Haven: Yale Univ. Press, 1981).

TENTH TO FIFTEENTH CENTURIES

Francesco Gabrieli, *Arab Historians of the Crusades,* selected and trans. from Arabic sources by Francesco Gabrieli, trans. from the Italian by E. J. Costello (Berkeley: Univ. of Calif. Press, 1969). [original title: *Storici Arabi delle Crociate*]

Gustav E. von Grunebaum, *Der Islam im Mittelalter,* (Zurich: Artemis, 1963).

Heinz Halm, *The Empire of the Mahdi: The Rise of the Fatāṭimids,* trans. Michael Bonner (Leiden and New York: E. J. Brill, 1996).

——, *Die Kalifen von Kairo,* Munich: C.H. Beck, 2003).
Maurice Lombard, *The Golden Age of Islam,* trans. Joan Spencer, new preface by Jane Hathaway (Princeton: Markus Wiener, 2004).
Hans Eberhard Mayer, *The Crusades,* trans. John Gillingham (Oxford and New York: Oxford Univ. Press, 1972 [1965]).
Adam Mez, *The Renaissance of Islam,* trans. Salahuddin Khuda Bukhsh and D. S. Margoliouth (New York: AMS Press, 1975 [1st English ed., London: Luzac & Co., 1937]).
Malcolm C. Lyons and D. E. P. Jackson, *Saladin – The Politics of the Holy War,* (Cambridge and New York: Cambridge Univ. Press, 1982).

FROM 1500 TO 1800

Abraham Marcus, *The Middle East on the Eve of Modernity,* (New York: Columbia Univ. Press , 1989).

THE NINETEENTH CENTURY

Albert Hourani, *Arabic Thought in the Liberal Age 1798–1939,* (Cambridge and New York: Cambridge Univ. Press, 1962 (reprinted numerous times).
Josef Matuz, *Das Osmanische Reich. Grundlinien seiner Geschichte,* (Darmstadt: Wissenschaftliche Buchgesellschaft, 1985).
P. J. Vatikiotis, *The History of Egypt from Muhammad Ali to Sadat,* (Baltimore: Johns Hopkins Univ. Press, 1969).

THE TWENTIETH CENTURY

Henner Fūrtig, *Kleine Geschichte des Irak,* (Munich: C.H.Beck, 2003).
Gudrun Krämer, *Geschichte Palāstinas,* (Munich: C.H.Beck, 2003).
Reinhard Schulze, *Geschichte der islamischen Welt im 20. Jahrhundert,* (Munich: C.H.Beck, 1994).

Notes on Pronunciation

Arabic names and terms have been transliterated in a form facilitating pronunciation for English-speaking readers. The macron always denotes a long vowel. If a word has only one long vowel, this is generally also the accented syllable. The *r* indicates an *r* rolled at the tip of the tongue, and the *gh* is a glottal *g*; *k* corresponds to the English *k,* while a *q* is a throaty, dark (velar) *k* (not *qu); kh* is pronounced like a hard *ch* as in the German *Bach*; *th* corresponds to the voiceless English *th* in *thing*, whereas *dh* is pronounced as a voiced *th*, as in English *the; s* is always voiceless, and *z* is always voiced. The *h* is always an audible consonant and not used to make a long vowel (e.g., *Mahdi*).

The right half ring, ' (hamza), indicates a glottal stop, whereas a left half ring, ' ('ayn), is a voiced pharyngeal fricative that is difficult for non-Arabs to pronounce. Since it is a consonant, words such as *Ka'ba or San'ā'* have two syllables.

Index of Names